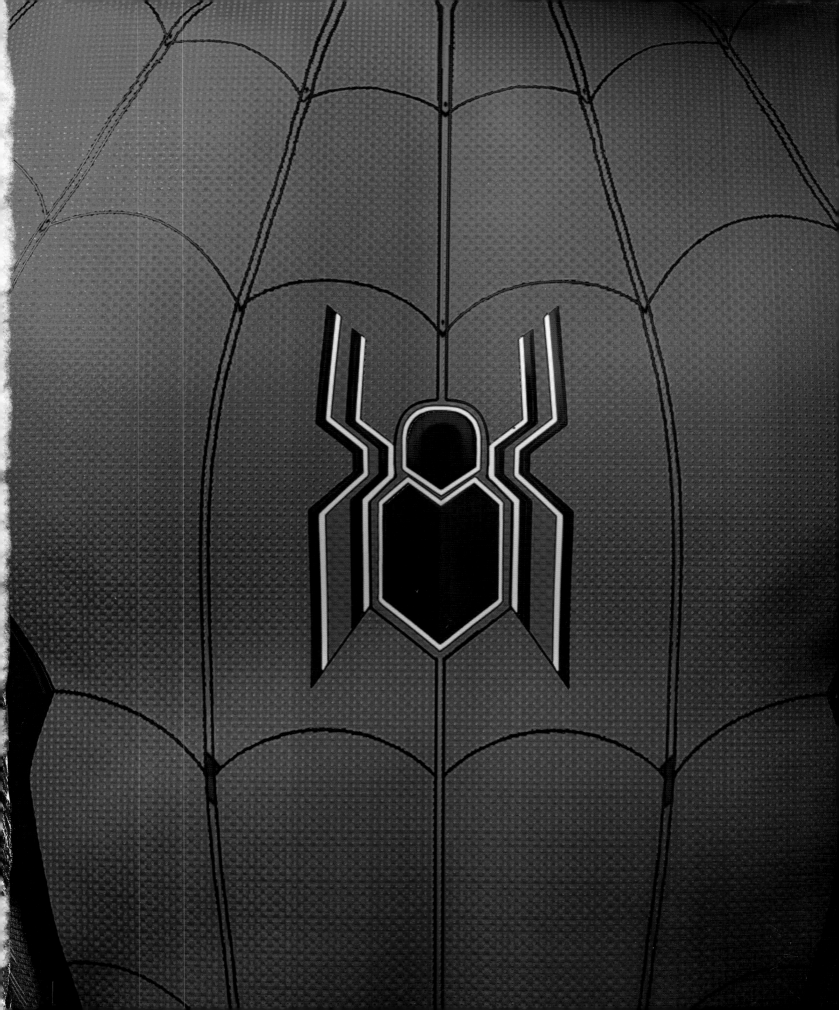

AVAILABLE NOW ON VARIOUS FORMATS INCLUDING
DIGITAL WHERE APPLICABLE FOR THE FOLLOWING FILMS:
Captain America: Civil War, Spider-Man: Homecoming, Avengers:
Infinity War, Avengers: Endgame, Spider-Man: Far From Home

Library of Congress Control Number 2021942301

ISBN 978-1-4197-4382-5

© 2021 MARVEL
© 2021 CPII
Book design by Liam Flanagan

Printed and bound in China
10 9 8 7 6 5 4 3 2 1

Abrams Books for Young Readers are available at special
discounts when purchased in quantity for premiums and
promotions as well as fundraising or educational use.
Special editions can also be created to specification. For
details, contact specialsales@abramsbooks.com or the
address below.

Abrams® is a registered trademark of Harry N. Abrams, Inc.

ABRAMS The Art of Books
195 Broadway, New York, NY 10007
abramsbooks.com

THE MOVIEMAKING MAGIC OF

MARVEL STUDIOS

SPIDER-MAN

WRITTEN BY ELENI ROUSSOS

A CINEMAGIC BOOK

ABRAMS BOOKS FOR YOUNG READERS
NEW YORK

SPIDER-MAN: NO WAY HOME
(2021) 125

AFTERWORD
THE FUTURE OF SPIDER-MAN 127

ACKNOWLEDGMENTS 128

FOREWORD

Everyone loves a good team-up.

Whether it's cheering on your favorite sports team, joining your friends online to play video games, or seeing your favorite Super Heroes join forces on the big screen at your favorite theater!

Many of us at Marvel Studios grew up loving the comic book–based movies that were around when we grew up. The excitement of seeing these larger-than-life characters leap off of the pages of our favorite titles and onto the big screen for the first time is a feeling I'll never forget. These films were also a big reason so many of us at Marvel Studios wanted to work in the film business to begin with. As spectacular as all those movies were, they all felt isolated. They were mostly movies about a hero, or team of heroes, who were the only heroes in their universe—who never got to cross paths with any other comic book characters from other movies.

However, at the end of the first movie set in the Marvel Cinematic Universe (MCU), Nick Fury told Tony Stark, that he was now "part of a bigger universe." And from that very moment, seeds were planted that set audiences' imaginations reeling with possibilities. Iron Man could meet Captain America. Thor and the Hulk could have an adventure on a strange, distant planet. And the greatest heroes on Earth could team up to form the Avengers. The potential for fun team-ups was seemingly endless! Any hero or villain could someday meet any other character in a movie—that's the fundamental idea that the Marvel Cinematic Universe was built on, and it was really exciting.

As cool as all this was, there was still someone missing. A character who people were uniquely excited to finally see interact with the other heroes of the MCU: Spider-Man! Even the very first issue of *The Amazing Spider-Man* comic featured Peter Parker teaming up with the Fantastic Four! Then, there is Spider-Man's literal introduction to the MCU, when he teamed up with Iron Man in Marvel Studios' *Captain America: Civil War*. Since then he's met, fought, or worked with Doctor Strange, Star-Lord, Black Widow, Falcon, Maria Hill, the Winter Soldier, and even Nick Fury himself, to name a few.

However, the story of Spider-Man joining the MCU is also the story of a lot of other team-ups as well. Team-ups that didn't happen in the fictional worlds of Marvel Studios films, or even on the pages of Marvel Comics. Team-ups that happened behind the scenes, in the real world—and without these team-ups Spider-Man wouldn't even exist, let alone have eventually been able to join the epic airport battle at Iron Man's side.

The first of these team-ups was when Stan Lee and Steve Ditko combined their talents to create what is now the most iconic superhero ever. Since then, scores of imaginative comic book writers like Dan Slott, Brian Michael Bendis, Gerry Conway, and Roger Stern have written tales of the web-slinger. And of course they worked alongside some of the greatest artists in the industry like John Romita (Sr. and Jr.!), Humberto Ramos, Todd McFarlane, and Mark Bagley—and this a wildly incomplete list. There are literally hundreds of talented authors and illustrators who've left their mark on Spider-Man's comic book legacy.

This is also the story of a couple of legendary producers, Amy Pascal and Kevin Feige, talking about how best to combine their efforts to bring Spider-Man back to the big screen. And perhaps more impressively, they convinced two major studios to work together to give Spider-Man new cinematic adventures unlike anything he'd had before.

On top of all that, creating a movie is an almost overwhelmingly staggering team-up in and of itself. It was my complete honor to join forces with my fellow producers as we collaborated with director Jon Watts and the Russo Brothers to help bring the amazing stories written by screenwriting teams McKenna & Summers, Markus & McFeely, and Goldstein & Daley to life. However, it is certainly not just writers, directors, and producers that make a blockbuster movie. Making a single film is already an incredible undertaking that can only be accomplished by teamwork. It takes hundreds of hardworking and passionate people to join forces to tell a story on the big screen. Its production designers and costumers. Directors of photography. Camera teams. Electricians and construction crews. Stunt teams and choreographers, along with drivers, caterers, and location scouts. There are production office staff, lawyers, and accountants. Safety monitors and health professionals. A single film even routinely employs pilots, scientists, and historians. And again, this is just a partial list. Without any of these people giving their amazing efforts to a production, you simply can't make huge movies like those people expect from the MCU.

I'll forever be thankful for the scores of sensational teams that paved the way for Spider-Man to swing into the MCU—and I'll be eternally proud and humbled to be counted among one of the many teams that were lucky enough to leave their mark on the legacy of Spider-Man.

Eric H. Carroll
Producer, Marvel Studios
Burbank, California
2021

INTRODUCTION

New York City, 1962—Two comic book legends, Stan Lee and Steve Ditko, create a brand new Super Hero for Marvel Comics. That hero? An unassuming teenager from Queens, New York, named Peter Parker. After a bite from a radioactive spider, he develops super powers overnight. With newfound skills like heightened senses, reflexes, and the ability to cling to walls— along with a brand-new costume and pair of web shooters—Peter Parker becomes Spider-Man.

That first appearance of Spider-Man in the comic *Amazing Fantasy* #15 captured the imagination of readers, and it was evident to Marvel Comics that fans wanted to see more of the web-slinger. Earning his own series, Spidey would carve a name for himself in the Big Apple and beyond. His popularity earned his way onto all sorts of merchandise over the decades, from clothing to toys, even garnering his own animated TV shows and

feature films. Spider-Man would eventually earn enough acclaim to make him the most popular comic book character in the Marvel pantheon.

Throughout this book, you'll find interviews that will help show you exactly how Marvel Studios creatives, concept artists, and freelance filmmakers reimagined the story of Peter Parker—as well as a host of supporting characters and villains—seamlessly bringing him into the Marvel Cinematic Universe. These pages, complete with concept art, storyboards, behind-the-scenes photography, and more, will show you exactly how Marvel Studios is further reinventing our beloved Spidey for a new generation.

Concept illustration of Spider-Man by Ryan Meinerding

LIST OF TERMS

The process of making a movie is divided into three phases:

PRE-PRODUCTION includes developing and writing the script, casting actors, hiring crew members, scouting locations to film, and designing and building costumes, sets, and creatures.

PRODUCTION refers to the actual filming, either at a faraway location or on a movie set (a large, hangar-like structure usually located on a movie studio property.) The cameras roll, the actors say their lines, and any practical effects are in place. This phase is also referred to as principal photography.

POST-PRODUCTION encompasses everything left to do once filming has finished or "wrapped." This includes editing (selecting scenes and putting them together to tell a story), sound editing and design (selecting and mixing the dialogue, music, and special effects), and visual effects, among other things.

KEY TERMS

VISUAL EFFECTS are all the visual movie elements that have to be created, either in pre-production or post-production.

PRACTICAL EFFECTS are physical rather than computer generated. They can be anything from simple props to pyrotechnics. They are filmed on set with actors. Practical effects include prosthetic makeup, animatronics, and on-camera explosions.

SCULPTS, MOLDS, AND CASTINGS are used to create everything from creatures to prosthetic makeup. A mold is a hollowed-out shape (think of a cake mold or ice tray). Molds are often filled with liquids that harden into three-dimensional shapes called casts. Casts are made of parts of the body that are called *lifecasts*.

Actor Tom Holland films a sequence in his Spider-Man suit for Marvel Studios' *Avengers: Infinity War*

PROSTHETIC MAKEUP is the bits and pieces (called prosthetics) added to an actor's face to significantly change his or her appearance. Prosthetic makeup is often created through sculpting, molding, and lifecasting techniques.

COMPUTER-GENERATED IMAGERY (CGI or CG) is a type of special visual effect created by a computer. The first 3-D computer images appeared in *Tron* (1982), *The Last Starfighter* (1984), *Young Sherlock Holmes* (1985) and *Willow* (1988). But it wasn't until the digital dinosaurs in *Jurassic Park* (1993) that CGI was deemed capable of creating photorealistic creatures.

MOTION CAPTURE is an effect in which an actor's movements are digitally recorded, then combined with character animation to create the final effect.

MAQUETTES are small-scale, three-dimensional clay models used for reference. They are sometimes scanned and then turned into CG creatures and characters as well.

GREEN SCREENS (also Blue Screens) are single color backgrounds used during filming. These screens allow visual effects artists to more easily replace backgrounds and add characters, props, and décor.

COMPOSITING (Comp) is the combining of multiple elements from various sources to create a final moving or still image. Example of this include background replacement, and the insertion of still or moving subjects/objects that were not present during a scene's filming into the final shot.

STORYBOARDS are drawings, like comic book panels, in which complicated sequences are broken down frame by frame to help filmmakers plan their shots. Sometimes these storyboard drawings are animated and edited to music, or sound effects, creating an ANIMATIC.

PRE-VISUALIZATION (Previs) is a rough 3-D animation of a film sequence. It is generally created after storyboards are made to help further conceptualize complex story beats and scenes before filming.

VISUAL DEVELOPMENT (Visdev) is an in-house department of artists at Marvel Studios. Their concept art helps conceptualize everything from environments, characters, props, and costume design. Often starting before a script is even written, they have helped provide a consistent voice in shaping the Marvel Cinematic Universe as a whole.

MARVEL STUDIOS

CIVIL WAR
CAPTAIN AMERICA

2016

The chance to bring Spider-Man into the Marvel Cinematic Universe came about in the 2016 cinematic adaptation of the comic crossover series written by Mark Millar titled *Civil War* (2006–2007). While that comic series focused heavily on the characters of Captain America and Iron Man, it also featured another major player—Spider-Man.

During pre-production, filmmakers discussed possibilities for integrating Spidey into the script. "If I recall, the idea that we could have Spider-Man as a Marvel Cinematic Universe character came up while we were developing *Civil War*, and the Russo Brothers jumped at the idea," says *Spider-Man: Homecoming* executive producer Jeremy Latcham. "They were so excited at the prospect of it."

"It's something that we at Marvel have been dreaming about for a long time . . . to bring Spider-Man into the context of the Marvel Cinematic Universe," says Marvel Studios' *Captain America: Civil War* executive producer Nate Moore. "Spider-Man got to join all of the Avengers in the same way that he has in publishing for years, so we couldn't be more excited."

"This *Civil War* opportunity really gave us a great 'in' to introduce Spider-Man to a new audience in a new context and clearly set up the rules," Latcham adds. "He's an MCU character. He's a contemporary of Tony Stark. . . . And that kind of idea that he's grown up in the Marvel Cinematic Universe is so different than anything that's been done with Spider-Man before."

Production illustration by Rodney Fuentebella

AIRPORT BATTLE

With Spider-Man coming into the MCU, the search for a new Peter Parker began. "Obviously there's a lot of pressure when you're recasting Spider-Man for the third time," Moore says. "We knew that if we were going to introduce Spider-Man into the Marvel Cinematic Universe it had to be special. So, we put on a very big casting search for the right guy for the job. . . . For us it was really important that we find a teen actor who both had the chops to be Peter Parker both now and in the future but also felt like a kid who could reasonably be in high school. And when we saw Tom Holland's audition, we were really blown away both by his physicality and by the earnestness and honesty that he brought to the role."

That physicality would come in handy when filming Spider-Man's first fight sequence in the MCU—a giant airport battle in which all the Avengers go toe-to-toe with each other. The filmmakers called this battle the *splash panel*—a term used in comics to denote a large-scale illustration in order to highlight either characters or dramatic action.

To help envision the splash panel, filmmakers relied heavily on visdev art, storyboards, and previs sequences. These same previs sequences would later serve as a guide for which camera angles and coverage were needed on set. "We spent months pre-visualizing the fight, basically going into the computer and

planning the attack," says Marvel Studios' *Captain America: Civil War* visual effects supervisor Dan DeLeeuw. "One of the biggest complications about a scene like this is the sheer number of heroes we have fighting each other. So when we're on set, we'll actually take a look at the previs as we shoot—our heroes will fight to the plan we created months and months before."

Peter Parker may be the most inexperienced fighter in the battle, but at the very least, he *looks* like he belongs, thanks to a brand-new suit courtesy of Tony Stark. While a physical suit was crafted for filming and actually shot on set, it didn't survive the post-production process. It was then that filmmakers redesigned the suit and visual effects layered a new costume over the practical one captured on set. Animation to the suit's eyes were also done during post-production, giving the final Spider-Man the ability to emote through the power of CGI. Filmmakers also utilized motion-capture (mocap) technology to help visual effects artists better depict Tom Holland's youthful portrayal of the web-slinger.

1 Splash panel concept illustration by Rodney Fuentebella

2 Splash panel concept illustration by Andy Park

3 Splash panel concept illustration by Andy Park

MARVEL STUDIOS

SPIDER-MAN
Homecoming

2017

Who needs an origin story? When it came time for Spidey's first solo film in the Marvel Cinematic Universe, filmmakers decided to forgo showing how Peter initially became Spider-Man. Instead, they relied on the character's popularity to inform audiences of past events. "A lot of people really know Spider-Man's origin inside and out," says producer Eric H. Carroll. "They know about the radioactive spider, they know about Uncle Ben—the whole thing—so rehashing that is not necessarily a priority because I'm not sure there's anything interesting to do with that per se."

By skipping Peter Parker's well-known history, it allowed filmmakers to explore a part of the character that had never really been done before on-screen—the juxtaposition between both his high school and Super Hero life. Taking inspiration from the classic John Hughes teen films of the '80s, like *The Breakfast Club* and *Ferris Bueller's Day Off*, filmmakers strove for an authentic portrayal of what it would be like for a teenage Super Hero to juggle his daily responsibilities.

"The goal of the Spider-Man franchise is not to save the world," explains executive producer Jeremy Latcham. "It's not to have the whole world at stake. It's not to have this Avengers-level conflict. The goal of Spider-Man, the thing at the end of the movie that should be at stake, is this kid's life. You know? His personal story should be what's at stake. . . . The real tension and stakes are about him and about doing the right thing. And obviously he needs to be a hero. Obviously, he's going to swing and he's going to do Spider-Man things, but the story could be a little more personal."

Art book illustration by Ryan Meinerding

HOMEMADE SPIDER SUIT

All Super Heroes have to begin somewhere, and that in-cludes a first super suit. Spider-Man's initial costume—a red and pale blue number—isn't flashy. This homemade suit was designed by Peter Parker himself, crafted with various resources a typical high school kid could get his hands on.

In reality, this suit was designed by Head of Visual Development Ryan Meinerding, who looked to the comics for its color palette inspiration. "There are runs in the comics where the blue on Spidey's suit is actually a lighter blue than the value of the red, and I just always loved that concept," Meinerding says. "The homemade suit was really based on trying to find a way of getting that color scheme with the powder blue and a really strong red, and using a Todd McFarlane spider on the chest. It just felt like a more innocent version of Spider-Man. And since Tom [Holland] was going to play an actual high school kid, it made sense having a suit that has an almost childlike innocence to it."

The homemade suit can first be seen on-screen in Marvel Studios' *Captain America: Civil War*—when Tony Stark shows up in Queens to recruit Peter Parker—but the design is more readily seen in *Spider-Man: Homecoming*.

STARK SUIT

What kind of Spider-Man suit do you get when its creation is left in the hands of a billionaire tech-genius? That's exactly the question filmmakers were trying to answer when designing Spidey's upgraded look.

Although this suit is chronologically Peter's second, it's the first costume he actually wears on-screen. With a design previously seen in Marvel Studios' *Captain America: Civil War*, this upgraded suit, courtesy of Tony Stark, helps to explain how a 15-year-old can get his hands on a beautifully crafted suit with extremely sophisticated technology. "We've always had to believe that Peter Parker would've invented this suit by sewing it on a Singer sewing machine and we just kind of went with it," producer Amy Pascal explains. "Now we don't have to do that anymore. Now Tony Stark's actually made him a suit that has all kinds of things, and all kinds of devices that Peter's going to discover."

"By doing that, we can say that this spider suit is super high-tech," says Carroll. "And it has all sorts of bells and whistles that something that he made himself probably wouldn't have."

1   Homemade suit concept exploration by Ryan Meinerding

2   Homemade suit concept exploration by Ryan Meinerding

3   Homemade suit concept exploration by Ryan Meinerding

4   Stark suit travel case with shrink-to-fit suit concepts by Ryan Meinerding

One of those new additions is found with his goggles, allowing Peter to convey his emotions while wearing the Spidey mask. "His eyes move—that's everything," Pascal says. "We have never been able to know Peter Parker inside the Spider-Man suit. We have never known what he's thinking. It's like Peter Parker disappears into a CG character and then you don't care. Now that character is going to tell you how he's feeling. Knowing how a character is feeling is everything. So, the action scenes are going to be about how he feels, and how I'm going to care about him when I watch them."

As the design of this suit, also courtesy of Meinerding, was completed during Marvel Studios' *Captain America: Civil War* post-production, it provided ample time for a physical suit to be constructed and worn on camera before filming began, making obsolete the need for a fully computer-generated costume for each on-screen appearance. For Spidey's animated eyes, filmmakers once again relied on CGI.

WEB SHOOTERS

You can't have Spider-Man without his webs, and his web shooters are an integral part of not only Spider-Man's costume, but his power set as well. For *Spider-Man: Homecoming*, two pairs of web shooters were designed—a bulky pair made by Peter Parker himself to go along with his homemade suit, and a sleek pair crafted by Tony Stark to complement his own Spidey suit design.

"The old-school web shooters are so cool," actor Tom Holland says of his homemade suit pair. "They're really big and chunky, they're really mechanical, and if you press the button, everything moves. . . . What I love about his original web shooters is they're as real as they could be. I know that's like impossible to make a thing that shoots web out of your hand, but the one thing with [the web shooters in] Andrew [Garfield]'s movie is that they were so small and so compact, it didn't really make much sense to me. But this is a big clunky thing that a kid would make in his room."

In addition to these old-school web shooters being built by Peter Parker, the web fluid contained inside each vial also sprung from his own mind. "Another thing we can really explore in these movies that wasn't maybe touched on as heavily in the older movies is that Peter is a very, very smart kid—like genius-level when it comes to science," Carroll explains. "So while the organic web shooters worked great in the original trilogy, we also think that demonstrating that he built the first version of his web shooters, and some of the other technological bits and bobs that are in his [homemade] suit really show off what a smart kid this is."

1   Homemade web shooter concept by Ryan Meinerding
2   Homemade web shooter brought to life by props department
3   Stark suit web shooter concept by Ryan Meinerding
4   Spider-Man tests the Stark suit web shooter in concept by Ryan Meinerding
5   Stark suit web shooter cartridges by John Eaves

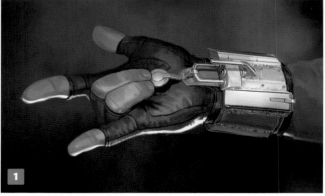

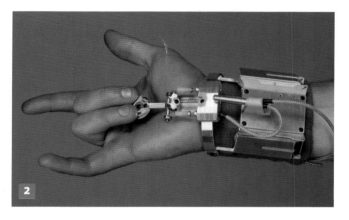

3

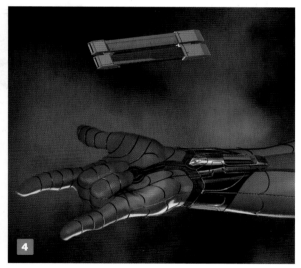

4

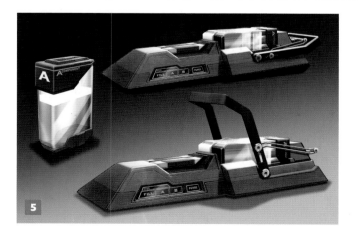

5

A different approach was taken when designing the Tony Stark pair. In addition to a sleek, black look, consideration was also taken with how the web fluid vials would appear. "When we started, we made everything opaque—and that had a really nice, clean look to it—but you couldn't see how the web shooters worked," concept artist John Eaves says. "The team wanted the cartridges to be clear so you could see the inside. They didn't want anything encased."

GAG & MOVEMENT SKETCHES

"When we told Ryan [Meinerding], 'Hey, there might be something to do with Spider-Man,' everybody on the Vis Dev team just flipped," Latcham says. "And there were so many designs so quickly because it's a bunch of guys who have always wanted to make Spider-Man. So, the amount of enthusiasm in the department when this kind of came around was staggering, right? Everybody wants to get involved, and everybody has ideas for Spider-Man."

Many of those ideas from the visdev department resulted in concept art gags—movement explorations for how Peter's new Stark-powered Spidey suit would either work (or not) while trying to perform his duties as a friendly neighborhood Spider-Man.

Movement exploration went far beyond just art reference like gags, storyboards, and previs. Tom Holland also informed much of the character's movement on-screen, performing many of the stunts himself under the watchful eye of stunt coordinator George Cottle and his team of experts. "[Tom] does things that are a little scary, and we encourage him not to [do those things] because, you know, you could hurt yourself," says Victoria Alonso, EVP of Production at Marvel Studios. "But, you know, as much as he can do, he will do. And whatever he can't do other CG will take over, or the stunt team will take him to fruition."

1 Concept sketches for Spider-Man by Iain McCaig
2 Movement concepts for Spider-Man by Ryan Meinerding
3 Spider-Man suit gags by Rodney Fuentebella

gas in hands misfires

3

HACKING THE SUIT

When Peter Parker decides to remove the tracker from his Stark-made Spidey suit—so Tony Stark won't know what he's up to—Peter discovers with the help of his friend, Ned Leeds, that his suit's full abilities have been restricted. Deciding to remove the *Training Wheels Protocol*, Peter unlocks a myriad of voice-activated abilities. These special features are executed by an AI assistant Peter decides to call Karen.

"Partway through the movie, Spider-Man realizes that there are a whole bunch of features on [his suit] here that Iron Man has disabled because he thinks he's protecting Spider-Man," Carroll says. "But Spider-Man thinks he's ready for all this power. So, he hacks into the suit and enables a whole other level of power that this suit has that Tony never told him about."

These unlocked abilities are displayed on a heads-up display, or HUD—a visual "screen" similar to the one Tony Stark has for his Iron Man armor—which can show information like diagnostics, location stats, and facial recognition data. Now unlocked to its full potential, Peter also gains access to 576 possible web shooter combinations like taser webs, ricochet webs, and web grenades.

1   A pre-production concept illustration of Peter Parker hacking the Spidey suit by Ryan Meinerding

2   Ryan Meinerding conceptualizes what the Stark-made Spider-Man suit looks like on the inside

3   Spider-Man HUD concepts by Rodney Fuentebella

4   Stark suit control panel concepts by Ryan Meinerding and Rodney Fuentebella

5   Spidey signal projector concept by Ryan Meinerding for *Captain America: Civil War* end tag/*Spider-Man: Homecoming* teaser

6   Spidey signal concept illustration by Josh Nizzi

7   Spidey signal projection and early design for *Captain America: Civil War* end tag/*Spider-Man: Homecoming* teaser

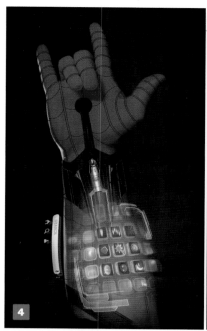

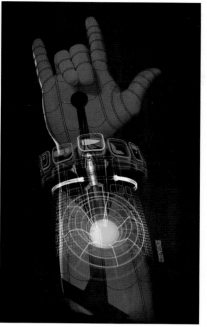

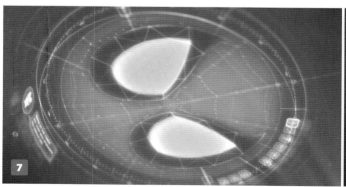

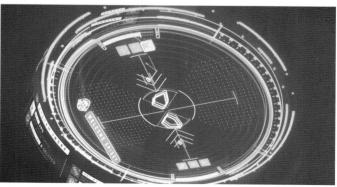

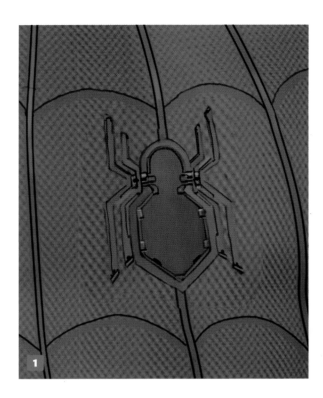

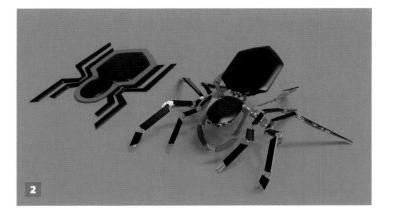

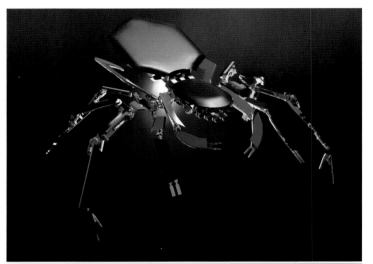

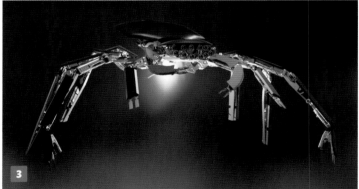

SPIDER DRONE

One of the unlocked features of Spider-Man's Stark-
made suit is a reconnaissance drone. The drone allows
Peter to see another vantage point through his HUD by
going where he can't go himself at that moment in time. The
drone is cleverly hidden on the front emblem of his suit.

"We all talked about the suit being designed by Stark,
and one of the running gags would be that it would keep
doing these things that he didn't know about, and have
these surprise abilities," recalls concept artist Josh Nizzi.
"The idea of the spider on the chest being a drone that
could pop out was one of them. So they really wanted to
have it be something that could fly, and wanted it to be like
a little buddy. We had to try to find that line—the drone is a
robot, but has his own AI—and determine how much personality to give him, but the overall idea made for a pretty
interesting design. It almost gives purpose for the symbol
being there. It's pretty ingenious."

1   Spider drone in its docked position on the front of
     Spider-Man's suit in concept by Ryan Meinerding

2   Deployed spider drone concept by Josh Nizzi

3   Deployed spider drone concept by Josh Nizzi

4   Deployed spider drone concept by Josh Nizzi

5   Light-up Spidey suit concepts by Rodney Fuentebella

EARLY IDEAS: LIGHT UP SUIT

Not every idea makes it to the final film. One idea explored by concept artists was a suit warning system for system malfunctions. As Peter's suit was now fully run by technology, it was conceived that his costume could experience glitches, stall out, or shut down entirely—issues Peter would never experience if he was wearing his homemade suit.

To explore these ideas, visdev artist Rodney Fuentebella conceptualized a myriad of possibilities. "I wanted to show that if the suit is having issues and going crazy, there could be some LED lights going off or something similar to visually let Peter know something was going wrong with the suit," Fuentebella explains. "Basically, if it goes off, something isn't going well at all."

In Marvel Studios' _Captain America: Civil War_, Tony Stark needed another member on his side for the upcoming battle against Captain America and his squad of heroes. Having discovered that a young kid from Queens might be the best "man" for the job, Tony recruits Peter Parker to his cause. Under the guise of a Stark internship—so Peter's aunt doesn't know—the young Mr. Parker is equipped with a new Spidey suit loaded up with all the latest Stark tech.

"A lot of the fun of the comics is always seeing different characters interact, and it happens all the time in the comics," Carroll says. "That's one of the things the MCU does so well is emulate what people love about the comics, but bringing it into a more realistic, plausible setting. And so it just felt natural. If we're going to have a Spider-Man set in the same universe as all the other Marvel movies, he's got to interact with a couple [of them], and who better than Iron Man?"

Including Tony Stark in _Spider-Man: Homecoming_ was a natural choice as the seeds of this pair's dynamic were already planted. When filmmakers approached Robert Downey Jr. to ask if he would be willing to have a major supporting role in the film, they were thrilled to hear _YES_.

"Tony kind of went and rolls up on him and says 'Hey, come under my wing,'" says Downey. "It's also kind of hugely irresponsible because they're finally playing Peter Parker as the young fella that he is. So, it's kind of odd and a little . . . dangerous and a little edgier and maybe a little irresponsible on Tony's part, but [it] seems like Peter can hold his own."

1 Character illustration by Phil Saunders

2 Concept illustration by Ryan Meinerding

3 Concept illustration by Ryan Meinerding

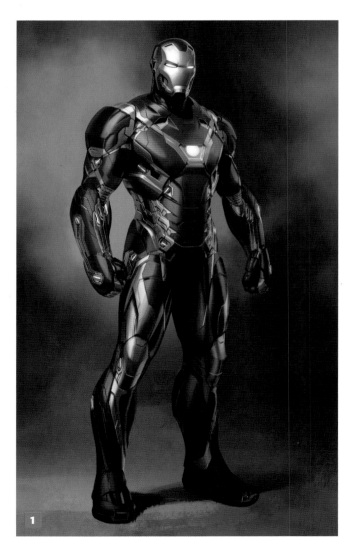

TONY STARK: MENTOR

Tony Stark, the self-proclaimed "genius, billionaire, play- boy, philanthropist," can now add mentor to his list of descriptors. "He definitely looks up to Tony," actor Holland says of Peter and Tony's relationship. "But I don't think he looks up to him in a physical way, in a way that like wow, what he's doing is really cool. I think he looks up to him because of how clever he is. And Peter and Tony are kind of on par with that kind of mindset. They have that very similar kind of wit. They're very funny—they're very fun characters—and I think he kind of sees him as a father figure in a way."

"A lot of the fun of Spider-Man is seeing this young hero interact with some of the older heroes," says Carroll. "When you're young, you have a different outlook on life. Things are a little more black-and-white. You operate a little less in the gray. Those are good guys. Those are bad guys. I know what's right. This is definitely wrong. And so putting Spider-Man in the MCU instantly gave us all these opportunities to put him next to guys like Iron Man."

HAPPY HOGAN

Portrayed by actor Jon Favreau, Happy Hogan becomes a middleman of sorts, observing and reporting everything Spider-Man does directly to Tony Stark. Being entrusted to watch over Peter Parker shouldn't be too hard of a task for him. Happy has been looking after his friend and boss, Tony, since the Marvel Cinematic Universe's beginnings with Marvel Studios' *Iron Man*. Wearing his self-imposed uniform of a suit and tie, Happy tells Peter, "I'm responsible for making sure you're responsible," and that's exactly what he does . . . or tries to do, at least.

MAY PARKER

May does what she can as Peter's sole caretaker. Unaware of Peter's Super Hero efforts and abilities, May fears the worst knowing that her nephew is constantly sneaking out of the house and leaving detention. It isn't until she accidentally sees him wearing his Spider-Man suit that she discovers the truth—that Peter is Spider-Man.

For the MCU version of Peter's aunt, May, filmmakers decided to make an unexpected casting decision, going with Marisa Tomei in the role. Traditionally, the role of Peter's aunt in both the film adaptations and comics has skewed older. "As fantastic as the portrayals in the previous films and comic[s] are, we . . . started saying, 'Well, wouldn't an aunt be more his parents' age? And wouldn't his aunt sort of be a little more like a big sister or someone much closer to him in age than has been sort of the classic in the comics?" Carroll says. "And then we just started trying to think of the best actresses we could think of in that general area. And, of course, Marisa Tomei was one of the first names that came up. . . . They have a very sort of older sister/ younger brother type relationship."

MIDTOWN SCHOOL OF SCIENCE & TECHNOLOGY

The Midtown School of Science and Technology prepares its students—and Peter Parker—for college and beyond. "One of the great things about Spider-Man in the comics is the importance of his everyday life in his adventures," Carroll says. "Spider-Man comics are always about how Peter Parker's life is affecting being Spider-Man and vice versa. And when you really look at the backdrop of high school, what you have is all that great soap-opera stuff, like, what girl does Peter have a crush on this week? Or does that girl like somebody else? And who's interested in who? And did he get his homework in on time? Or was he out crime-fighting too late? And I think the backdrop of high school gives a lot of dramatic opportunities there that make it feel different than the other Super Hero movies."

Filmmakers were adamant that the fictional home of the Tigers would be as diverse as its real-life inspiration school—the Bronx High School of Science in New York City. "When it came to casting the roles that surround Peter Parker in this movie, we went to New York City schools and just looked around and said, 'What does it look like?'" explains Carroll. "And there is literally no template for a New York City school. They're all over the place. There's every race, shape, and creed of kid at pretty much every

school in New York. So we just said, 'Great, there's no types for any role. Let's just literally find the best actor for each part. We don't care how tall they are, how short they are, what body shape they have, their race. Let's just find the best kid.' And in so doing what came together is this cast that I think really looks like a general New York City school population."

As Peter attends a magnet tech school, the rules are different than one would expect from a social perspective. "Being nerdy and geeky and techy doesn't make you an outsider," director Jon Watts says. "It makes you cool and popular, or an entrepreneur. So what I think we're going for is it becomes more of a personal thing. It's less of like he fits into this clique, or he doesn't fit into this clique. It's more just his own insecurities that sort of put himself outside of the other groups and cliques at school."

The exterior of the school was filmed at Franklin K. Lane High School in Brooklyn, New York. The school interiors were shot in Atlanta, Georgia. Even though these shots weren't filmed in the Big Apple, filmmakers still strove for an authentic New York feel. "The main reference we used for the interior was Brooklyn Tech High School," production designer Oliver Scholl says. "That was our favorite. It is a huge school in New York. We just loved the feeling of the interior in terms of the equipment, the posters, the student artwork—walking through the school there was just a very upbeat lively look to it. However, we couldn't match the architecture in the school we ended up using [for filming] in Atlanta."

1   Actor Tom Holland as Peter Parker easily leaps the fence surrounding his school thanks to wires which were later removed in post-production

NED LEEDS AKA THE GUY IN THE CHAIR

5

Ned Leeds would love nothing more than to play with Lego blocks and watch *Star Wars* with his best friend, Peter Parker. When Ned discovers that Peter is Spider-Man, all he wants to do is help his friend with his Super Heroing in any way he can. Eventually, Ned asks to be his "guy in the chair"—someone who assists a Super Hero via a headset, and helps by looking up important things that the hero can't find out himself at that point. "He's such a comic book nerd," actor Jacob Batalon says of his character. "He's so into heroes. And all he wants to do is just be a part of it. And so, when he finally finds that out [that Peter is Spider-Man] it's just like the greatest thing in the world for him. . . . He wants to do everything. He wants to help out.

He wants to save people. It's crazy. His enthusiasm is what really drives me personally."

1 Hanging up banners in preparation for the homecoming dance in concept illustration by Henrik Tamm

2 Exterior of homecoming dance in set illustration by Richard K. Buoen

3 Inside the homecoming dance, students party the night away in set illustration by Richard K. Buoen

4 Spider-Man looks longingly through the glass outside of the homecoming dance in concept illustration by Ryan Meinerding

5 Director Jon Watts goes over script sides with actors Jacob Batalon and Tom Holland

MICHELLE "MJ" JONES

Quirky student Michelle always seems to have her nose in a book. While she may seem like a bit of a loner, she's always around, randomly inserting herself into conversations. "I'm not going to lie—she's weird, but she's super cool to me because I feel like she's constantly thinking about something," says actor Zendaya. "She just kind of sits back and observes and then randomly says little things. And you're like, 'what?' But usually what she says is very true and very real. . . . She's just like an old soul. And I feel like she's always kind of on a different mental wavelength than other people."

"Zendaya herself really informed what we did with the character of Michelle," Carroll says. "And so in this school full of really smart kids who do homemade robotics and build computers at home in their spare time—she's the kid walking around school always with some kind of novel or paperback book in her pocket."

When Michelle takes over as the new captain of the Academic Decathlon Team, she lets her peers know that her friends call her MJ.

1 Rough character concept of Ned with Spider-Man and
Iron Man by Ryan Meinerding

FLASH THOMPSON

Ever since Spider-Man's first comic book appearance in 1962, Flash Thompson has been bullying Peter Parker. While the Flash of the past was more aggressive in his treatment of Peter, the Marvel Cinematic Universe version of Flash, played by actor Tony Revolori, employs more mentally manipulative tactics. "[Peter] goes to this school full of really smart kids, so Flash is more of an academic rival than just a bully who's picking on him because he's a nerd," Carroll says. "In fact, Flash is a smart guy, too, and his main beef with Peter is that it seems that Peter has to work a lot less hard to get good grades or be on the academic decathlon team. . . . What Tony Revolori did really well for the character of Flash is show this sort of cocky on the outside but a little insecure on the inside version of the character."

LIZ ALLAN

Peter Parker has a major crush on fellow decath-lon teammate and high school senior Liz Allan. While Liz can tell that Peter likes her romantically, it's not something that she initially takes very seriously. "A cool senior isn't going to date a nerdy sophomore," says actor Laura Harrier, who plays Liz. "It just doesn't happen in the realm of high school. But after the thing at the Washington Monument, after almost dying [and] after being saved by Spider-Man, I think she was like, you know, screw that. Like why do I care what these people think of me in this like silly high school world? If I think Peter's really smart and interesting, and he is cool, and if I feel something for him why not go for it and follow up on that? I think she really comes into herself and starts to figure out who she is and what her priorities are and where she wants to fit in in the world and relate to other people."

Eventually, Liz agrees to go with Peter to the homecoming dance. When Peter goes to her house to meet up before the dance, he discovers that Liz's father is the very man he has been trying to apprehend as Spider-Man—the Vulture.

COACH WILSON & MR. HARRINGTON

The ever-caring and concerned Mr. Harrington, played by actor Martin Starr, is always eager to help his students in science class. As coach to the Academic Decathlon Team, Mr. Harrington takes his squad to the national competition in Washington, D.C., where they not only win the title but also get saved by Spider-Man.

Physical Education teacher Coach Wilson, played by comedian Hannibal Buress, always looks like he would rather be anywhere else besides the high school gymnasium. When not prepping his students for Captain America's Fitness Challenge, he can be found supervising detention.

PRINCIPAL MORITA

Principal Morita takes his job as the head of Midtown Science seriously. He's always making sure there is order in the hallways. Strong-willed and unafraid to send kids to detention, he's also willing to give students a second chance if they deserve it.

Discerning fans may pick up on clues that Principal Morita is related to another character in the MCU. Do you know who?

ANNE-MARIE HOAG

Anne Marie Hoag—played by actor Tyne Daly—is the dir-ector of the Department of Damage Control. This organization was created to handle all post-battle cleanup and salvage operations immediately following the Battle of New York—when the Avengers teamed up to fight the alien Chitauri invasion.

The creation of Damage Control, led by Hoag, ended up disrupting various salvage contracts issued by the city—including that of Adrian Toomes and his team. By taking away the livelihood of those contractors, Damage Control inadvertently led those hardworking individuals to seek other, less-than-legal ways to earn a living.

Including Damage Control in the Marvel Cinematic Universe—an organization that already existed in the comics—finally gave filmmakers a way to address some of the fallout after these major battles. "One of the things that hit us early on as we were talking about developing the picture was this notion that there's all this tech out there in the world, and it's all kind of falling to the ground through the cracks in the MCU," Latcham says. "You know, Chitauri fall out of the sky in New York. Tony Stark blows up 40 Iron Man suits in a bay in Miami, and they all sink to the bottom of the ocean. Who's gathering all that stuff? What's happening to all of it? . . . Well, what's fun about having a group like Damage Control taking all this material, destroying it all, cataloguing it all, storing it all is that there could be a leak. Some of it could not get destroyed. Some of it could be sinking through to the people."

PHINEAS MASON
AKA THE TINKERER

One of the members of Adrian Toomes's old salvage operation is Phineas Mason—also known as the Tinkerer. While messing around with some Chitauri alien tech, Phineas was able to discover that it had great potential. Over the years he was able to adapt and craft the tech into many uses—most notably weaponry, which his old salvage group sells on the black market. The Tinkerer is played by actor Michael Chernus.

1 Set Illustration of the Tinkerer in his lab by Richard K. Buoen

TINKERER TECH

Many of the initial black market weapons and tools fashioned by the Tinkerer were based off of Chitauri alien tech—but why stop at salvaging items from one catastrophic, Marvel Cinematic Universe world event, when materials could come from other places too: A cosmic convergence with Dark Elves descending onto Greenwich, London. Helicarriers being shot out of the sky and crashing straight into the Potomac. The Battle of Sokovia, where a city was literally ripped up from its foundations—filmmakers simply had to follow a cinematic path of destruction for inspiration. "What happens if you take some of that stuff," says Latcham, "then you piece some stuff together, and it's all high-tech materials, and you take it and you build a suit of armor out of it? That would be pretty cool. What happened to all those [sub-]Ultrons that blew up at the end of *Age of Ultron*? Well, if those pieces are starting to get sold on the black market and they have tech in them, maybe there's pieces of exotic metals. And who knows what else is available? You start piecing it together, you get somewhere. And so, we've kind of come up with this notion that there's a weapons bazaar and that there's an under-

ground market and that there's these dealers trading in MCU relics that are all out there in the world."

To get their hands on the materials, Toomes and his men tap into an entire criminal network. "They're stealing stuff off the back of trucks," Latcham explains. "And it's working guys who drive a truck or who work at a construction site who call—and they know if they call a guy, who calls a guy, who calls a guy—that someone shows up and gives you a nice check. And you got rid of this Chitauri tech that you were going to send off to get destroyed, and you made a nice little pretty penny [in the process]. . . . It was a fun way to get into creating new villains."

For the black market goods, production designer Oliver Scholl strove for a man-made look with an alien feel—mixing the metals and plastics of earth with materials seemingly not from this world. "We went through the armory at ISS [Independent Studio Services, which supplies props to film and TV productions] and picked out about 20 different rifles, and showed them to the director and to Oliver [Scholl], and they picked three or four out of there," recalls concept artist John Eaves. "What we needed

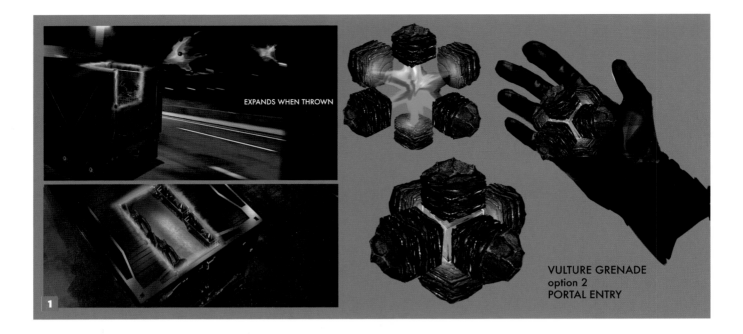

EXPANDS WHEN THROWN

VULTURE GRENADE
option 2
PORTAL ENTRY

to do was take those rifles and add, in the . . . Chitauri stuff from [*Marvel's*] *The Avengers*—with that gold, blue, and organic sheeting. That added sci-fi element gives a kind of mystical power source. Something that could turn a human-made invention like a gun into something a little bit more powerful. We had to keep that gold color between what would be man-made and what would be Chitauri. So, we used darker weapons, like black ones, as opposed to stuff that is more camouflaged. They really wanted a high contrast between the two materials."

Tinkerer tech can be found all over Toomes's Bestman Salvage. A few pieces, however, get their own chance in the spotlight. One tool that is used during a pivotal scene in the latter part of the film is the ferry cutter. "We looked at chainsaws and concrete cutters and we started to manipulate that with the Chitauri stuff," says Eaves. "The concrete cutter had a really cool look. It was something that was portable that they could carry in with a handle, so it worked really well. For the cutter itself, in the beginning, the plan was to design two practical blades with the Chitauri stuff on it, and when it would spin, it would generate this kind of laser cutter, but that didn't end up in the final version."

Physical versions of the various Tinkerer tech were constructed for filming, but for the otherworldly effects emerging from these weapons and tools, filmmakers relied on CGI.

1 Chitauri portal grenade prop concept by John Eaves
2 Prowler glove prototype concept by John Eaves
3 Ferry cutter shown both on and off in concepts by John Eaves

AARON DAVIS

Another potential black market buyer, Aaron Davis, hits up Toomes's crew to buy some tech. During the deal, Jackson Brice started shooting into the sky, demonstrating some of their items. This attracted the attention of Spider-Man, who eventually interrupts the exchange. Concerned about a potential setup, Toomes's crew flees the scene with Spider-Man in tow, leaving Davis behind.

Eventually, Davis is tracked down by Peter when he uses his Spidey suit's facial recognition capabilities. Unintimidated when his interrogator, Spider-Man, showcases his lack of experience in soliciting information from criminals, Davis—out of concern for his nephew—decides to tell Spidey where Toomes and his crew are going to be next, giving the web-head a new lead.

Aaron Davis is played by actor Donald Glover.

MAC GARGAN
AKA SCORPION

Mac Gargan, played by actor Michael Mando, is a potential black market buyer. He has a distinct scorpion tattoo on his neck. Having been ensnared in Spidey's webs during a black market deal gone wrong on the Staten Island Ferry, Gargan is arrested and sent to prison. In *Spider-Man: Homecoming*'s mid-credits scene, the now imprisoned Gargan chats with Toomes, vowing to find out who the man behind the webbed mask is—and kill him.

In the comics, Mac Gargan—the Scorpion—is one of Spider-Man's oldest adversaries, first appearing in 1964's *The Amazing Spider-Man* #19.

Two more members of Adrian Toomes's salvage-operation- turned-criminal-enterprise are Jackson Brice and Herman Schultz. Brice and Schultz—played by actors Logan Marshall-Green and Bokeem Woodbine, respectively—both sell the black market weaponry created by Phineas Mason to the criminal underworld.

Brice, with an affinity for a specific gauntlet created by the Tinkerer, tries to convince his crew to call him the *Shocker* due to the powers of the weapon he wields. While moving merchandise, Brice is reckless, often firing weapons indiscriminately to showcase the power to potential buyers. Fed up with these public displays—and the potential of bringing too much unwanted attention to their operation—Toomes fires Brice from the group, fully willing to let him leave the operation peacefully. Unfortunately, Brice reacts poorly, threatening to undermine their operation. This causes Toomes to dissolve their relationship—literally. With the incinerated Brice no longer needing the shocker gauntlet anymore, Toomes gives Schultz the gauntlet, making him the new Shocker. Schultz, now wearing the shocker gauntlet, fights to protect their black market operation.

Even though the Shocker's design in the comics is very costume-y, concept artists still found a way to give a nod to his roots. "For the Shocker, we wanted to not make it seem too much like a costumed character, but still be inspired by the original Shocker from the comics by giving him the same lines, coloring, and texture schemes," says concept artist Rodney Fuentebella.

Knowing that the Shocker weapon would need to be a creation of the Tinkerer in this story, filmmakers once again looked to a previous entry in the Marvel Cinematic Universe catalog for inspiration. "We also repurposed Crossbones' gauntlet from Marvel Studios' *Captain America: Civil War* into that Shocker look," says Fuentebella. "Since a lot of the bad-guy tech comes from repurposed items that were stolen from other movies, we figured this could be another item that was altered."

1 Shocker gauntlet prop illustration based on Crossbones gauntlet by John Eaves

2 Character illustration of actor Bokeem Woodbine as the Shocker by Rodney Fuentebella

3 Shocker pounds Spider-Man through a school bus in concept illustration by Richard K. Buoen

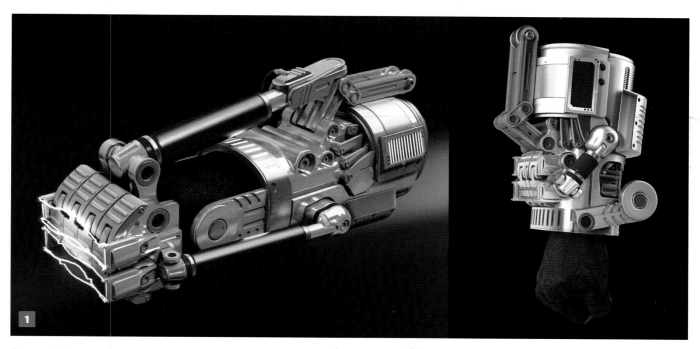

ADRIAN TOOMES
AKA VULTURE

Adrian Toomes—also known as the Vulture—led a salvage operation that was displaced by the creation of the Department of Damage Control shortly after the Battle of New York. Needing another means of income and seeing a financial opportunity in Phineas Mason's alien-tech creations, Toomes recruits his former coworkers for a team that steals and repurposes advanced technology, eventually reselling it on the black market for a hefty sum. "[In] Super Hero movies there are always villains, and I suppose he serves that purpose," says actor Michael Keaton of Adrian Toomes. "But we pick my character up when he is a hardworking guy who has built up this pretty great business. He's doing quite well. He may not be wealthy, wealthy, wealthy, but he's doing all right, and he works hard. And to simplify, it could be described as a scrap metal business. . . . Then, mandates and orders come down that would now be under the auspices of a larger agency, and basically wiping him out. The thing that I used as my driving interior kind of motivation—not to sound too actor-y—but the

question that is in his head is probably a really good one, which is where's mine? You know? I think he sees it above and beyond Tony Stark. When they all have theirs, where's mine? I've been working for mine. You've taken this from me. So he says I'll figure out where to get mine."

To get what Toomes believes is his and his men's right, he has the Tinkerer craft a tool to help them steal more high-grade technology—a massive winged exo-suit. This helped filmmakers bring a practical design perspective to the outlandish costume the Vulture wears in the Marvel Comics. "The idea that you would just build a suit to look like a vulture is very showboat-y, and somewhat old-fashioned," says Watts. "I think there's an element to that we can touch on, but for me it's more of why you would need a wing suit in the first place. And if you can come up with a good reason for him to need a wing suit, then it's just working backward from there. Why is this real? Why would you have this? Why do you need to fly up to a certain height? If you fly up to a certain

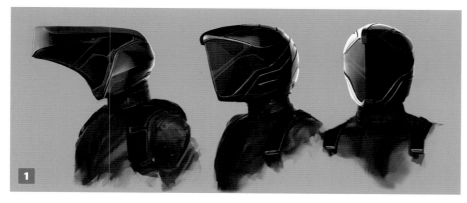

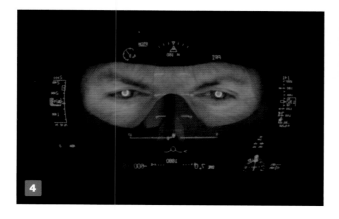

1 Early Vulture character mask illustrations by Ryan Meinerding

2 Character illustration by Josh Nizzi

3 Vulture flight suit illustrations by Rodney Fuentebella

4 Vulture HUD display by Josh Nizzi

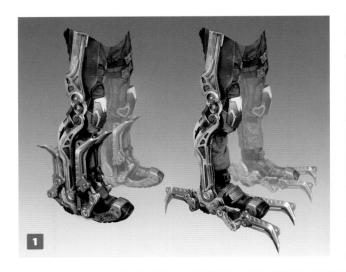

1   Retractable Vulture talon concept by Phil Saunders

2   Vulture exo-suit harness concept by Josh Nizzi

3   Vulture exo-suit concept illustration by Josh Nizzi

4   3D model of Vulture exo-suit and figure by Paul Ozzimo

5   Spider-Man dodges Vulture blades in early concept illustration by Josh Nizzi

height, would you need a helmet? Do you need something for when there's no oxygen when you get to high-altitude levels? Do you have to stay warm? Is this military technology? Or is it this a hacked sort of thing that the Tinkerer has built? How many personal embellishments would you put on this if it was basically custom-made for you? So I think within that world, you get to have a lot of fun with why it looks the way it looks."

The Vulture's look is best analyzed in two parts—the base costume and the full winged suit.

Toomes wears a brown aviator jacket with fur trim on the base level of his costume. This not only allowed filmmakers to tip their hat to his aviation ways while flying in his full look, but also gave them a clever way to bring over the fur collar from the comic design. With a very old-school militaristic look planned for the costume's bottom layer, it only made sense that filmmakers used materials to match. "The first fabric we looked at for the Vulture ended up being too shiny," Frogley says. "The final trousers were made from actual 'new' old-stock World War II fabric. It was beautifully colored and proportioned, and looked absolutely perfect for the character. Sometimes wonderful fabric does exist, it's just hard to get ahold of."

For his winged suit—complete with exoskeleton and helmet—filmmakers were adamant that their Vulture designs didn't bear any resemblance to that other winged character from the MCU. "One of the things we were trying to figure out as a start-

ing point was how do we make it different from Falcon," recalls Meinerding. "And there have been some other winged characters on-screen over the last little while. Looking at the comics is usually a place that we start, but his look in the comics has been *so* inspired by bird wings that it didn't feel like a strong enough place to start. So we ended up looking at trying to think of him as somewhere between Falcon and a vehicle. So it wasn't just a guy with a set of wings flapping his arms around, but it ended up feeling like the wings were imposing and powerful enough on their own, and that he was sort of plugging into it. And that is when the scale started to make more sense—because a vulture is a big bird, too, thinking of it as being all very large with the wingspan. Falcon's wingspan is about 12 feet, and Vulture's, I think is about 36 [feet], so that was probably the place where it started making the most sense in trying to make him feel compelling, and interesting and cool."

"So the wings got larger and the suit got bigger," says concept artist Josh Nizzi. "And it really kind of set it apart from the Falcon stuff. I think a lot of it was trying to find the balance in the design, and trying to find poses that could work with the mass. The wings had to have enough articulation in them so that they could get into these poses where he could fight Spider-Man one-on-one, and not always be flying around in the air like an airplane. And because of how it's articulated, you can still kind of get that Vulture shape and then allow the wings to fold up or hang down."

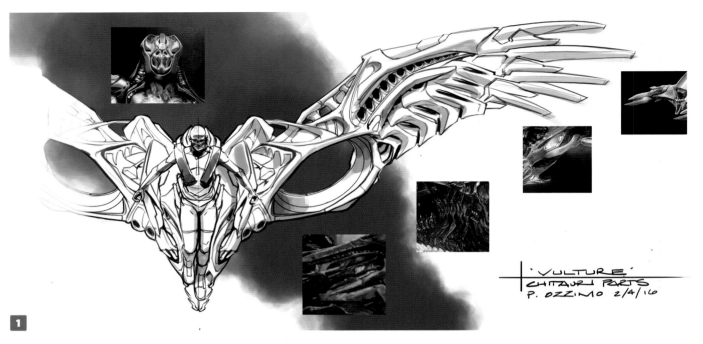

1

2

3

While filmmakers were aware that the winged portion of the design would need to be created using CGI, the exoskeleton frame and helmet were planned to be practical effects. "One of the things that knocked me out about being the Vulture was the amazing artistry from the people who built the Vulture suit," says Keaton. "It was extraordinary—down to the tiny little nuts and bolts. . . . But just what they made, the artistry and even the mechanics of it, you know? I was just knocked out by how talented those people were."

The Vulture's high-tech headgear was based off of the F-35 Joint Strike Fighter helmet. "[Those] helmets have this thing where there is eye-tracking on the face shield, and they have these green lights that project over the pilot's eyes—so it's kind of riffing off this technology," says Nizzi. "If he's flying at night, it can be kind of like night-vision goggles, and of course it can help convey the green color of the Vulture from the comics. It's a bit menacing. The outer green is also reflected inside the mask on

the HUD display. It's also a little sinister in the way it highlights his face."

For the onset helmet, SCPS designers worked to make sure the glowing green eyes would not negatively affect the actor's performance, allowing them to see from behind the glowing-green lights easily.

1   Vulture concept sketch by Paul Ozzimo
2   Vulture concept sketch by Anthony Francisco
3   Vulture character illustration by Josh Nizzi

ANATOMY OF A SCENE

ATM ROBBERY

The first time Peter Parker encounters black market tech on the streets of Queens is during a bank robbery. After using a cutter to slice open the front of an ATM, the criminals utilize an antigravity gun, easily discarding the heavy, metallic casing. These tools, which have been modified with Chitauri tech by the Tinkerer, enable the thugs to grab the money inside with relative ease. Unbeknownst to them, Spidey is watching their every move. The web-head eventually confronts the criminals—who are all sporting different plastic masks of the Avengers—and a fight ensues.

"At one point there's money flying in everywhere like one of those cash tornados in a casino or something," Carroll says. "And in the end, one of the guys sets loose this crazy laser cannon thing that just rips the roof off the building next door—which is the bodega he always goes to

after school to grab a sandwich at. So he rushes out there to help this guy, but by the time he gets back, the thugs are gone with their tools and a little bit of money."

To film the scene, filmmakers modified existing structures to fit their needs. "That sequence, even though it is set in Queens, was actually shot in Atlanta," Scholl explains. "We dressed an intersection into our deli and ATM/bank. The ATM was an empty building that we completely took over and we just built our space into it, and the deli used to—funnily enough—actually be a bank that we changed to fit our space. Basically, for the ATM bank to integrate all the stunt rigging above the ceiling into the actual physical location was quite an achievement from the rigging team. All of the effects were physically built into the fans and ceiling. We tried to get as much as possible in camera [practically]."

WASHINGTON MONUMENT

1

Inside the Washington Monument, Peter Parker's class- mates and teacher are trapped in a damaged elevator. Knowing that he is their only hope, the wall-crawler puts on his Spidey suit and springs into action to save his friends. Quickly ascending the Monument's façade, Spider-Man climbs higher and higher.

Atop the white obelisk, Peter gazes across the horizon, careful not to look down. He's never been this high before. "One of the ideas that always excited us is that heights are scary," Carroll says. "This Spider-Man isn't irrationally afraid of heights, but afraid of being high off the ground the way any normal person like you or me would be. So when the writers of the first draft, Jonathan Goldstein and John Francis Daley, pitched us the concept of Spider-Man having to climb the Washington Monument—which is not only really tall, but there is nothing to web onto around it if he falls or gets into trouble—this just felt like a great way of making the audience fear for Peter's safety."

Peter eventually musters enough courage to swing through a small window at the top to get inside—just in time to save his friends from falling toward certain doom.

Unable to film the exterior and interior shots needed for this sequence at the real Washington Monument, sections had to be recreated on soundstages. "The whole monument was split into several pieces for filming," Scholl says of the multipart set. "The top of the Monument was on a stage. We had a separate setup where it was just the elevator in front of a green screen for the traveling shots. And then we had the base of the Monument with the entrance and base of the elevator shaft."

1 Concept illustration by Ryan Meinerding of Washington Monument with cutaway of top deck for filmmaker reference

2 Concept illustration by Josh Nizzi

1

Overall, having to build the Monument themselves gave filmmakers greater control over their environment. The exterior structure was built at a slight pitch to allow actor Tom Holland—assisted by wires—to climb up the faux exterior with more ease. Other benefits included greater allowances for things like camera placement and framing. "We ended up building the space I think 25 to 30 percent bigger just for the camera to feel right, and for Spider-Man to be able to move around and to have the action take place," explains Scholl. "We did something that is pretty faithful, to a certain extent, to the original [Monument design]. The glass panels on the walls are something that really exist there. We made it a tad bigger because of the action. We cheated the whole space bigger."

For the interior of the Monument, the same sizing considerations were made. "The elevator cabin, it's eight-by-eight-foot, size-wise, I think," says Scholl. "We just laid it out so it would have enough space for the kids to be in there, and again for moving around [with the camera]. Because we are actually still on a stage with a 40- to 50-foot-high ceiling—and we have everyone in the air—there are a lot of safety concerns. And so being on the stage and being able to control that [environment] is actually really important—to make sure that everyone is safe."

To streamline the pacing of the sequence, another change was made to the Monument's interior. "In the real Monument, there is another lower floor that has a museum space," says Scholl. "We didn't build that into the set because it adds another layer of complication to the elevator plot that wasn't necessary."

The filming of the elevator set took close to a week. "We shot the elevator sequence—the explosion and the elevator dropping multiple times and being pulled back up, etcetera—and you really see how they've crafted it almost like à comic book—[how] they've crafted each piece," says actor Martin Starr. "They've like fully laid out everything and animated most of what they want of that action sequence. I don't know if you've seen anything like this before, but they animate it all [in previs]. So then they shoot the exact same clip, put it into that animation. And they're just kind of replacing, beat by beat, how they saw this entire action sequence going. It's pretty interesting."

1   Concept illustration by Josh Nizzi
2   Concept Illustration by Peter Rubin

FERRY RESCUE

"The producers, Jon Watts, and I were sitting in a room with the writers, and we were like, 'Wouldn't it be cool if we could split the Staten Island Ferry in half?'" Carroll recalls the origins of this action-packed sequence. "It's just one of those ideas where you think you're going to get into that meeting, and people are like, 'Uh, well, I don't know'—and of course [special effects supervisor] Dan Sudick's the kind of guy who's like, 'Yeah, sure, I know exactly how we're going to do that. We're going to build it up on these struts. We're going to have hydraulics to split it in half. I'm going to put three giant dunk tanks behind it.' And he delivers every time."

The first step filmmakers needed in recreating the Staten Island Ferry was obvious—research. "We tried to pull as much information about the Ferry that exists," Scholl says. "We actually got some models of the ferry to put on the conference table, and the team took a look and discussed what it would take to achieve a practical look. What time, money, and all that would make sense? When we were discussing this sequence, we also didn't know if we would get permission to shoot on a real ferry, so we also had to build most of the ship in order to actually shoot parts of the sequence—not just for the physical action of ripping apart the ferry."

"Oliver Scholl and [supervising art direction] Brad Ricker and the rest of the art department are fantastic," says Carroll.

"They have taken painstaking notes, looked at every blueprint available to them, scanned the actual ferry, toured the actual ferry dozens of times at this point, and then worked with our construction supervisor John Hoskins to just build this amazing 60-foot set. . . . It's really pretty impressive. But when you're on there, too, and you're walking around, I mean—it's the details down to the sprinkler system in the ceilings. It's all there. They brought it [all]. It's accurate. It's amazing."

The final ferry set was built on top of hydraulics, tilting and moving the set in a way that actually splits the ferry in half. Dunk tanks sit behind, pumping a few thousand tons of water through the set, with stuntmen safely rigged on the boat to toss them around—all captured directly on camera. "[Shooting practically] just gives it such an epic sense of scope and scale for the actors, for the crew," Carroll adds. "They know what they're trying to match, even the parts of it that we'll be augmenting with CG will be so informed by what we're actually doing here. You just can't predict exactly what water's going to do—what a giant four-story boat is going to do when it gets crashed [by waves] and separated in half—and [the ferry], it was built in a way so that when it cracks in half there wasn't already a seam. So little pieces in the floor actually were torn up and popped and cracked. And, again, it's just the kind of stuff that you can't simulate."

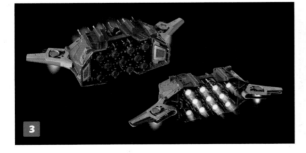

1   Concept illustration by Josh Nizzi
2   Concept illustration by Henrik Tamm
3   Stark mini repulsor drones encased in larger
    drone pod concept by Josh Nizzi
4   Mini repulsor drone concept by Josh Nizzi

PERSONAL MOTIVATION

FILMMAKERS OFTEN FIND INSPIRATION FROM THE pages of Marvel Comics—in the characters, their costumes, in even the action found on the panels themselves. That was the case with a sequence right before the epic final battle, when Spider-Man finds himself trapped under an enormous pile of rubble. Unable to move the objects above him, Peter musters all his strength, cheering himself on in the process, to escape. "It seems like it's hopeless," Carroll says. "The weight is just too much for this poor kid, and he can't budge it—which comes straight out of the comics, *Amazing Spider-Man* #33—and Spider-Man knows if he doesn't get out of there, lots of bad things will happen to a lot of good people. After panicking a bit, he realizes he doesn't need help, he doesn't need Iron Man to save him. He finds the strength within himself to lift off the tons of concrete and steel on top of him so he can go stop the Vulture."

1   Concept illustration by Ryan Meinerding
2   Concept illustration by Ryan Meinerding
3   Interior page from *Amazing Spider-Man* #33 (1966) scripted
    by Stan Lee and plotted/penciled/inked by Steve Ditko

BATTLE IN THE SKY

A giant cargo plane thousands of feet in the air moving at 500 miles an hour—that was the stage filmmakers wanted for the epic final battle between Spider-Man and the Vulture. To complete this sequence, it would need to be 100 perecent digital—unlike the scenes at the Washington Monument or Staten Island Ferry—in order for filmmakers to pull this off.

To make this fully CGI sequence look as real as possible, visual effects vendor Sony Pictures Imageworks worked tirelessly to ground the battlefield—especially the wings and fuselage—in reality as much as possible. The final plane design would be covered by over one million flexible LED panels, creating a video screen around the entire airplane. The images projected on these screens would come from the surrounding environment, cloaking the vehicle when airborne. As the fight gets more intense, sparks, fire, and the characters themselves can also be seen reflected in these panels. For Spider-Man's movement, mocap and other performance footage assisted animators in recreating actor Tom Holland's subtle movements, helping reaffirm the illusion that it was really him inside the Spidey suit.

1　Concept illustration by Peter Rubin
2　Concept illustration by Henrik Tamm
3　Concept illustration by Alexander Mandradjiev
4　Concept illustration by Alexander Mandradjiev
5　Concept illustration Ryan Meinerding

MARVEL STUDIOS
AVENGERS
INFINITY WAR

2018

You can't be a friendly neighborhood Spider-Man if there's no neighborhood," Peter Parker tells Tony Stark, hoping it will be enough—enough to convince Tony to let him help save the universe.

Although reluctant, Tony agrees. He'll need all the assistance he can get in the battle against Thanos. "What makes Thanos so great is that his conviction and his belief in that this is the only way; there is no other solution," Co-President of Marvel Studios, Louis D'Esposito says. "He's seen it firsthand on his planet. And he's doing what needs to be done for the greater good. So with that kind of conviction and that kind of belief, it really makes a powerful villain."

Iron Man and Spider-Man are not alone in their goal. Trying to stop Thanos are a myriad of other Marvel Cinematic Universre characters, many of whom are sharing the screen for the first time. "You can feel the excitement, even with the crew, when Chris Pratt walks out and does his first scene with Tom Holland and Robert Downey Jr.," says President of Marvel Studios and Chief Creative Officer of Marvel Kevin Feige. "It is pretty amazing. Or when Chris Hemsworth as Thor encounters the Guardians for the first time. There is just something chemically awesome about seeing these different franchise heroes interacting with each other for the first time. And when you think about it, we haven't really seen that since the first Avengers film. *Avengers: Age of Ultron* introduced some new characters within the body of that film. Marvel Studios' *Captain America: Civil War* introduced Black Panther and Spider-Man within that film, which was great and awesome. But there is just something at a deep, human level that is satisfying about the notion of seeing characters you've grown to love in their own movies walking into another movie for the first time."

"I think that's the biggest part of this particular movie—to see them all integrated into one and seeing them banter with each other," Executive Producer Trinh Tran says.

Concept illustration by Ryan Meinerding

SENSING DANGER

The Iron Spider, first teased at the end of *Spider-Man: Homecoming,* finally gets worn in Marvel Studios' *Avengers: Infinity War.* The Marvel Cinematic Universe version of this suit is also created by Tony Stark.

Besides having built-in nanotechnology and spider legs, the suit also allows Peter Parker to breathe in space. "[It's] something different—something that he can breathe in," co-director Joe Russo says. "Something that will let him function in the environment he's about to encounter."

To design Spider-Man's new suit, filmmakers once again turned to Meinerding. "I think for me, some of it is looking at the language we're trying to create, and then really just understanding the new journey they're putting him on in the movies," says Meinerding of designing looks for Spider-Man. "I think a lot of the effort that goes into the storytelling is trying to find new experiences, new environments, new problems, new challenges for him to face—with the most obvious challenge being actually treating him like a teen in high school. So how can that new suit reflect those journeys? And then also tapping into the language that we started on Marvel Studios' *Civil War* and finding ways to riff off of the stuff we've done in previous MCU movies becomes a very valid source of inspiration, almost as much as from the comics."

Designing the Iron Spider came with its own set of unique challenges. "The choice to do the legs in the movie did not come about upfront," Meinerding says. "It was essentially, 'Let's do an Iron Man–based Spider-Man suit.' So I was doing versions of that and trying to find a happy medium between a Spider-Man suit and an Iron Man suit, and it was only later that the decision to actually put the legs on it came in. . . . I think he definitely feels like a different Spider-Man in this movie. It allows him to feel like he's moving away from being just a friendly neighborhood Spider-Man and actually becoming an Avenger—which is a huge story point, and one that I was happy to help contribute to."

For filming, actor Tom Holland wore a mocap suit, with the final suit design—spider legs and all—added using CGI.

1 Character illustration by Ryan Meinerding based on the classic Iron Spider design as it appears in *Amazing Spider-Man* #529 (2006)

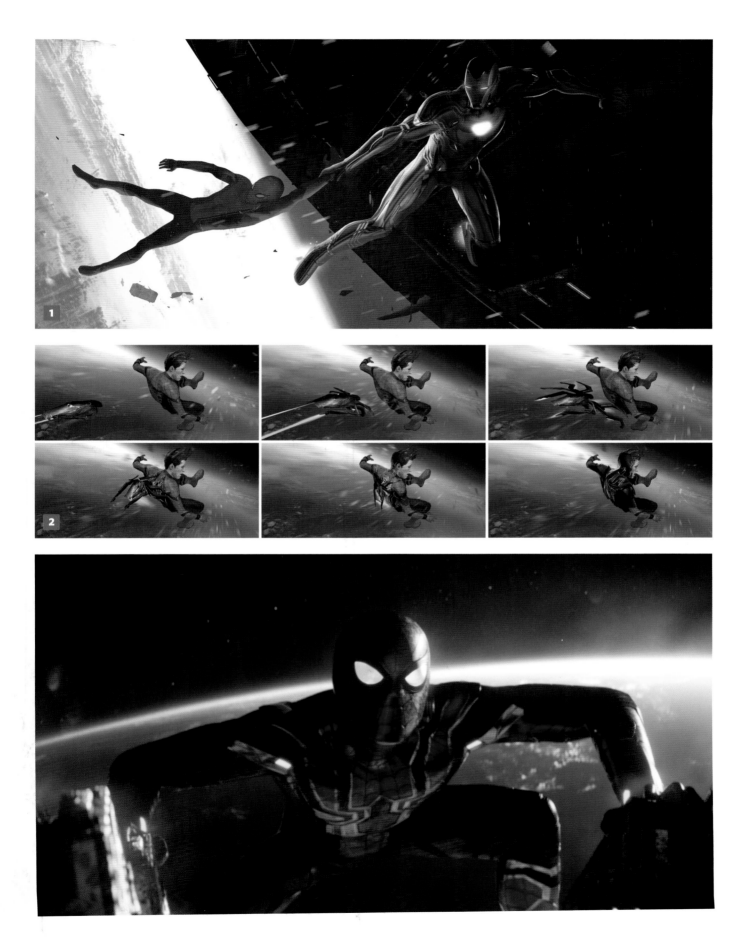

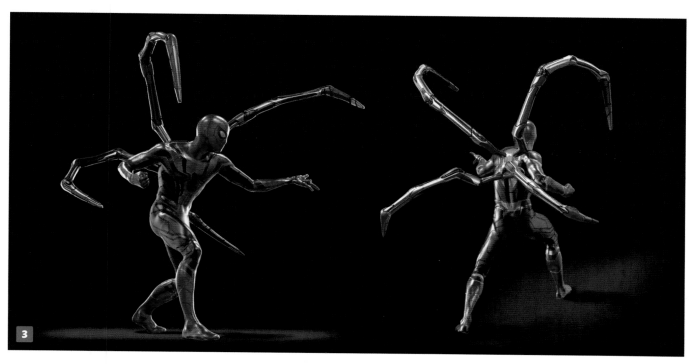

1   Iron Man grabs Spider-Man before he falls back to Earth's surface in concept illustration by Stephen Schirle

2   The Iron Spider suit deploys and assembles onto Peter Parker in concepts by Rodney Fuentebella

3   Iron Spider character illustrations Ryan Meinerding

4   Iron Spider 3D model concepts by Ryan Meinerding and Adam Ross

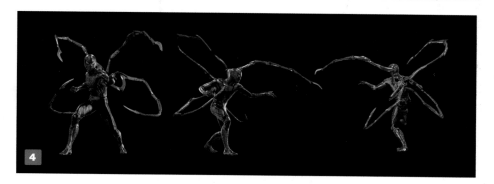

SPIDEY ON TITAN

Deciding to bring the battle to Thanos instead of waiting for him to find them, Tony Stark, Peter Parker, and Doctor Strange head toward Thanos's birth planet. It is there that they meet the Guardians of the Galaxy and plan a team-up, hoping to take him down once and for all. Thanos soon returns to his former home world of Titan—a dusty land covered in the ruins of a once-vibrant civilization—ready to battle for possession of one of the Infinity Stones and to bring him one step closer to his ultimate goal. "It's no mistake that we get to Titan the way we get to Titan, right?" Alonso says. "I mean, Iron Man has been battling—for six years now—the shadow of Thanos, and he has a choice. Doctor Strange says, 'Can you get us back to Earth?' And Tony Stark says, 'Yes, I can, but I won't because all along I've been waiting for this moment, and I'm not going to walk away from it. I am going to go head-on, and we are going to go battle this guy.' Now, they don't know what they're about to encounter on Titan. They don't know that it's a desolate environment. They don't know that there's no life there. They don't know that they might not find Thanos. So with the help of Spider-Man,

the three of them get there, and it is truly a conscious choice of saying, 'Instead of walking away from what has been haunting me all along, we're going to go. We're going to face it, and we're going to defeat it. And if nothing else, we're going to try.'"

The battle on Titan, which was the first scene filmed during production on Marvel Studios' *Avengers: Infinity War*, saw Peter Parker's inaugural fight as an Avenger, against the biggest bad guy in the universe. "What [actor] Josh [Brolin] did with that character was incredibly difficult in a way of how minimalist everything was that he did," says Holland of Brolin's portrayal of Thanos. "It's quite difficult when you're doing mocap, especially when you're mocapping a character who's eventually going to be eight feet tall and a big, purple titan. . . . Josh did such a still, simple performance that he was almost scarier in how calm he was. And I just think that that technology has become so advanced and so incredible, and it was just a breath of fresh air to see someone transform like that in front of our very eyes and then to transform on-screen and become Thanos. It was pretty remarkable."

BATTLE ON TITAN

Thanos obtains all the Infinity Stones, and with a snap of his fingers, half of all living creatures in the universe disappear. "My favorite part is seeing how invested everyone is in these stories and these characters, to the point of this movie really having affected people," Meinerding says. "I think that having Thanos win, and losing characters that people love, and the shock that went along with that—especially when Spider-Man went—it was incredible. I'm not saying that it's a treat to participate in something that made people sad, but just to help be part of the MCU that people are so invested in—that they're on this roller coaster of a ride with sort of [cinematic] universe storytelling and seeing how it all plays out and watching those emotional connections pay off—it's some-

thing that I would have never thought I would have been able to participate in."

It wasn't just audiences that were affected by the loss of their favorite characters. The heroes that survived the blip would also become overwhelmed with grief, especially Iron Man. "The relationship between Peter Parker and Tony Stark is integral to the emotional core of the film," co-director Joe Russo says. "And it's one that was set up in [Marvel Studios'] *Civil War*, continued in *Homecoming*, and is furthered here. And it is a father-son relationship, and one that will ultimately end up being exceedingly painful for Tony. As snarky as his relationship is with Peter Parker, he cares deeply about him, and to have him die in his arms is will change him forever."

MARVEL STUDIOS

AVENGERS
ENDGAME

2019

Audiences were stunned when the Guardians of the Galaxy and Earth's Mightiest Heroes had failed at the end of Marvel Studios' *Avengers: Infinity War*. Thanos had collected the Infinity Stones and destroyed half of all living things in the universe with a single snap—including many beloved characters from the MCU. Deciding who lived and who died was no small task. "We were very meticulous at picking exactly who we wanted to survive Thanos's blip," Tran explains. "We really wanted *Infinity War* to be Thanos's movie and have *Endgame* really be about the heroes—and especially about the heroes reuniting. And if you think back to the first *Avengers*, it was that feeling of the core Avengers coming together, forming as a team—reuniting and putting aside their differences so that they can come together for the common cause of fighting the bad guys—and it's in essence a little bit of that with *Endgame*."

Each surviving hero reacts to the loss in a distinct way. "All of the remaining heroes deal with the events at the end of *Infinity War* differently," Feige says. "All of them are used to trauma of one kind or another. None of them are used to being defeated so thoroughly by a single antagonist, and I think they are trying to figure out how that happened and why that happened."

Peter's death weighs heavily on Tony Stark's conscience, becoming one of the main reasons why he helps to bring everyone back. "As a recovering sociopath, Tony is—he's not all that touchy-feely, but we know that he is pretty crazy about this kid," says Downey. "And I think [Tony] really appreciates the crucible that he went through as we saw in *Homecoming*, and then obviously the continuation of that in *Infinity War*. So, I suppose there is a sense of—whether you are or not—if somebody believes you're a mentor, or a figure to them of some projection, ultimately it can be a good thing because it can make you strive to be a better person."

Concept illustration by Ryan Meinerding

THE RETURN OF SPIDER-MAN

Actor Tom Holland, who is notoriously bad at keeping secrets, often had the filmmakers keep relevant information from him so as not to inadvertently spoil major plot points for audiences. This resulted in confusion when filming Marvel Studios' *Avengers: Infinity War* as he wasn't given an entire script. Instead, Holland relied on sides—pages of the script that cover what is being shot that day—to piece together his own story arc. "I remember reading the sides before I even knew anything about the blip, and I genuinely thought they just killed me off," says Holland of his character. "I was like, 'Well, I have two more movies to make. What the hell, guys?' So, I honestly thought they'd killed me off for some reason. And then I found out that there was going to be a fourth *Avengers*, and we'd all come back, and we'd save the day in some, way, shape, or form. It was pretty tough carrying the world's biggest secret for six months or whatever that press tour was because everyone wanted to know—and the one thing I *did* know about the movie was the biggest spoiler of the whole movie. So, it was just really difficult for me to keep my mouth shut—and I did. I was really proud of myself. I actually did not spoil anything."

To bring everyone back after the blip, the surviving heroes need to obtain all of the Infinity Stones. Eventually, the Avengers would succeed in collecting them all, gathering together to witness Hulk give a "snap" of his own, reversing what Thanos did five years earlier. "[We] asked ourselves often, 'What does it mean to bring everybody back?'" says screenwriter Stephen McFeely. "'What is the best way to do that?' We certainly tried a version where everyone came back, and you knew it immediately, and there they were. Maybe they all came back to wherever you wished them to come back to, and then Thanos attacked them all at once, but doing that prevented us from a really heroic reveal."

For the big reveal, filmmakers relied on the magical rules established in *Doctor Strange*, unveiling our heroes on the Earthen battleground all at once through dimensional gateways. Peter Parker, emerging through a portal with the other fallen heroes from the Battle on Titan, is a welcome sight to Tony Stark—earning Peter a hug from his mentor.

FINAL BATTLE FOR THE UNIVERSE!

With Thanos and his alien army poised to annihilate the planet, all of our heroes are eager and ready to put an end to Thanos and his schemes once and for all. "This final battle in itself is a movie," Tran says. "We have pretty much everybody, all of our heroes, all in one scene. In the beginning, we envisioned this moment where they're all in one shot, and we pan over, and you see every single hero in the Marvel cinematic history all in one frame as they're coming out of the portals. And as soon as Steve Rogers utters those words, 'Avengers assemble'—I mean, it sends chills to my body because that's the most exciting moment for audiences to see. But to be able to have them all come together, and they charge, and they're ready to go, and they know that this is their one opportunity to stop the bad guy—it's pretty incredible."

"We wanted to do a great finale that not only had the spectacle worthy of what they were left with at the end of Marvel Studios' *Infinity War*, but with sequences and scenes and character interactions that could only be done with a crew of people that has been working together as long as we have, with a group of actors that has been portraying and embodying these characters as long as our actors have," Feige says.

"[Co-director] Joe Russo has described this a couple of times as 'strange alchemy'—of putting disparate characters together and seeing how they can interact," Meinerding recalls. "And when you have characters that were never really meant to share a film frame together all of a sudden doing so, that means you just open up opportunities for creative fight scenes and interactions."

For Spider-Man's part of the battle, Tom Holland was able to appreciate the full use of virtual production—a type of real-time computer graphic technology—which instantaneously layers CGI models over captured footage, better allowing filmmakers to visualize the final look. "It gives us that creative freedom to push ourselves to the limit and really come up with some cool, interesting stuff," says Holland of the process. "So, for this, working with the Russo Brothers, it's been really fun because no idea is too crazy in a mocap volume. You can say, oh, midway through this scene can I stab an alien in the face with my i-Spider legs? And [they're] like, 'Yeah, that's absolutely possible. So, let's give it a go.' And then you can see it almost instantaneously with the rendering that's so quick. So, it's pretty magical. And I can see how in the future it'll take over and become such a huge part of our industry—as it already has—but will grow even more."

Concept illustration by Ryan Lang

1 Spider-Man runs with gauntlet and is assisted by Groot in storyboard concept frames by Rodney Fuentebella

2 Spider-Man turns Groot into a slingshot in concept illustration by Jackson Sze

3 Spider-Man is launched over great distances thanks to a combined effort of both Giant-Man and the Hulk in concept illustrations by Ryan Meinerding

4 Spider-Man is freaked out by alien Miek laying eggs in storyboard concept frames by Jackson Sze

1   Concept illustration by Phil Saunders

MARVEL STUDIOS

SPIDER-MAN

Far From Home

2019

Five. Years. Later. The casualties of the blip have been made whole again. The newly resurrected—like Peter Parker—return to a different world than the one they left. For those that disappeared, time moved on without them. The world moved on without them. Everything changed.

Peter Parker—who rapidly transformed from *normal kid* to *Super Hero* to *Avenger*—longs for a simpler time. He wants a break from responsibility. He wants a break from being Spider-Man. "He's experienced some astounding things," Feige says of Peter. "He's encountered many different characters. Having come back to Earth—figuratively and literally—after that, to get back to school, and to get back to *your* life. And that's what he wants more than anything. He wants to get back to his life, and he wants to grow up. And he wants to have some semblance of a normal life, and events of the film start to prevent him from doing that. And how is he going to face them? Does he embrace this huge responsibility that's put on his shoulders, or does he want to try to step away from it? And that's the struggle we find in him."

Peter contemplates his heroic future as he travels all over Europe with his classmates on a school trip.

While traveling in Venice, Italy, Nick Fury actively recruits Spider-Man to fight a new threat—and *No* is not a word Fury will accept for an answer. For Peter, it seems that wanting a "normal" summer with his friends is too much to ask. "Spider-Man to him has become a bit of a chore," Holland says of his character. "He decides to sort of hang up the suit and go on holiday and enjoy his time with his friends, and just be a young adult and be someone who's enjoying their life and learning who they are and finding out where they belong in the world. But throughout the course of the movie he realizes he's already found out where he belongs, and that's in the Spider-Man suit. And that's with the responsibility of saving his neighborhood and saving the city and in some cases, saving the world."

Concept illustration by Ryan Meinerding

FRIENDLY NEIGHBORHOOD HERO . . . AGAIN

Spider-Man isn't as clumsy in his suit as he used to be. He's found a certainty in his newest armor—the Iron Spider suit—since helping to save the universe. "He's really come into his own as a hero," Carroll says of Peter Parker. "He's still that lovable kid trying to find his place in the world that we know and love from the earlier movies, but he's a little more confident in his skin. He knows how to use his powers to better effect. He's more comfortable with the tech that Tony gave him, so he's really found his stride. And of course, what we want to do as filmmakers is knock him off his stride a little bit and see how he deals with it this time around."

As a solo hero in the Marvel Cinematic Universe, Peter Parker predominantly fights low-level crooks in his Queen neighborhood. However this time, the enemies Peter faces challenge the web-slinger in new ways. "In the first Spider-Man movie, we saw him come up against a bunch of really grounded, street-level bad guys, and that is part of what people loved about that film," Carroll says. "So we don't want to go too far from that, but we do want to make sure Peter is coming up against threats that seem bigger and scarier than the ones he faced in the first movie—and maybe even ones he understands a little less."

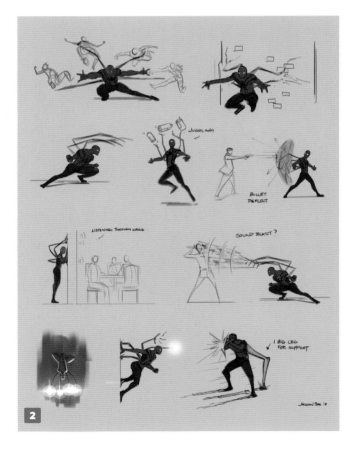

1   Spider-Man stands atop the Battle of New York monument in concept illustration by Henrik Tamm
2   Spider-Man movement sketches by Jackson Sze

MAY PARKER

Five years after Thanos's infamous snap, May Parker blipped back into her Queens apartment only to find another family living there. Deciding to help other families who have been displaced by the blip, May uses her nephew's heroic alter ego—which she discovered at the end of *Spider-Man: Homecoming*—to help her raise money for the cause. "What's great about having someone like Marisa [Tomei] playing May is she brings a playfulness to the character," Watts says. "She's just smart and she just sort of radiates this kind of intuition. So, in the last movie, she knew something was going on with Peter even though she didn't know specifically what it was, she wanted to help. And now that she knows his secret, I think we really are going to get to see a side of their relationship that we've never really seen before in the movies."

Since May discovered Peter was Spider-Man, she has come to accept his ability to help others, and even encourages it. May is somewhat romantically involved with Happy Hogan, although they both define the relationship differently when confronted by Peter.

HAPPY HOGAN

Happy and Peter's relationship has evolved since *Spider-Man: Homecoming*. "They have much more of a rapport, and the way they interact definitely demonstrates that they've become really good friends," Carroll says. "There are a few big differences—first and foremost, of course, they are still dealing with the loss of Tony. Happy lost his best friend; Peter, his mentor. That's huge, and it is the sort of tragic event that really forges special friendships. The other wrinkle is that Happy and May seem to have taken a romantic interest in each other. Peter loves them both, but it can't help but get awkward as he tries to navigate the idea that Happy and his de facto mom are dating."

MICHELLE "MJ" JONES

MJ is always paying attention. Her intuition and curiosity lead her to a major discovery—that Spider-Man is none other than fellow classmate and friend, Peter Parker. "MJ's pretty smart," says Zendaya. "You know, she kind of knows what's going on even though she could care less about it. If there's anything I know about her as a character is that she's like very, very perceptive. And also, she's like a bit of a detective. So, she's constantly watching everyone even when they don't think that she's watching. She knows what's going on. So, when she figures out about Peter's secret, we kind of see it coming. It's like she watches everything. She knows everything."

Throughout the film, MJ proves that she's not only smart, but can also take care of herself and others. She is no damsel in distress. "She's saving herself," says Zendaya. "She's helping her class get to safety. She's definitely not just waiting there for him [Spider-Man] to come fix everything. You know, she is actually the one who helps him figure out what's going on and actually solves the case—really—so, without her, who knows what would happen? . . . I think that's important, especially for young women, you know? To be able to see that, and just different forms of female characters. It's important for us to see ourselves in different ways on-screen. So, I'm glad that they made that point."

A BLOSSOMING ROMANCE
PETER & MJ

Peter Parker has a crush on MJ. Deciding that this summer trip is the perfect chance to tell her how he feels, he devises a plan. But no amount of planning and calculation can help Peter find the right moment. Love—especially young love—is tricky. "In this film, we wanted to create the most idyllic version of what summer romance is," Holland says. "And realistically it's very awkward. You always see in films when they fall in love instantly, and they're head over heels for each other, and it's easy. But in reality, there's lots of walking in silence and thinking about holding each other's hands, but being too nervous to and stuff like that. And we really honed in on that—the awkward teenager side of love."

Prague becomes the perfect setting for Peter to finally tell MJ how he feels. "Prague is such a beautiful city," Carroll says. "Whether day or at night—but at night, especially—you get all these great vistas of the castle on the hill, the bridges all lit up, all these beautiful churches and ancient buildings that are just so beautifully preserved. There's something about this city at night that really has a romantic feel."

1   Black dahlia necklace concepts by Christopher Caldow

NED LEEDS & BETTY BRANT

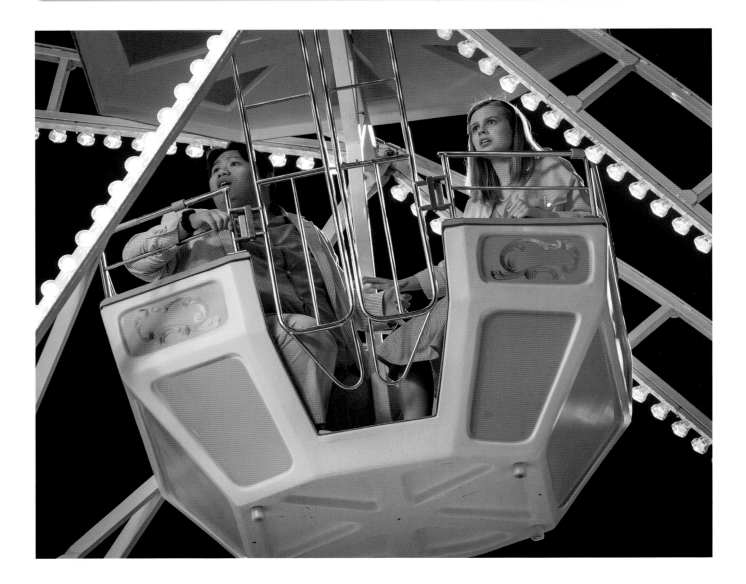

Ned Leeds, Peter Parker's best friend, has a plan for them this summer—he wants them both to be bachelors in Europe. Although Ned is unattached when the plane to Venice takes off, he has a girlfriend by the time he lands—classmate Betty Brant.

"I feel like Ned kind of brings out the fun side of Betty," actor Jacob Batalon says. "Betty is always like on the go, she's about her work only, and she's just straightforward. She doesn't want to have too much fun, all that stuff, and she's very prim and proper. And Ned just—he's just here to have fun and have a great time. And I feel like that's like the best thing about them. They just bring out the best in each other."

"I think she's very hardworking," actor Angourie Rice adds of her character. "She's a very diligent person. She wants to get the most out of high school that she can, so that's why she signed up for this trip. But a lot of unexpected things happen along the way. She gets together with Ned—Peter's best friend—and so they're kind of the couple on the trip, and that's very exciting for the both of them. They do everything together."

Even though the two of them seem smitten with each other throughout their trip through Europe, by the time the film is over, Ned and Betty mutually agree to end their relationship and remain friends.

FLASH THOMPSON

Peter Parker's academic rival, Flash Thompson, loves all things Spider-Man. "The dichotomy of him loving Spider-Man and hating Peter Parker—I think that's great," actor Tony Revolori says. "It creates a great bit of comedy in an otherwise big action movie. And I think that's really cool to just have those moments where you could say I love Spider-Man and then screw you, Peter."

Like many teens, Flash lives on social media, documenting and live-streaming his European holiday. "Playing Flash, we really tried to figure out a way to make him as relatable as possible, while also this not being you," Revolori explains. "[And] what it came down to was basically trying to personify an Internet bully, or someone who has anonymity through his actions and words. . . . You'll notice him in this movie being very similar to . . . vloggers who are a little bit out there. They're all for their fans. And he's Instagramming everything for his Instagram followers and this and that and whatever. And it's really great. And he has a little bit of a shining moment toward the end of the film where he reveals how insecure he really is, only to get validation from Happy Hogan, played by the great and wonderful Jon Favreau."

BRAD DAVIS

Out of all the featured students on the Midtown summer trip, Brad Davis is the lone snap survivor of the bunch. Originally five years younger, Brad now finds himself the same age as classmates like MJ, Ned, and Peter. "He's described by [Ned], one of the other characters, as being that kid from five years ago who always got these nosebleeds and cried all the time, but then all of a sudden, you know, he's grown up," actor Remy Hii says of his character. "There was a blip that happened, and five years went by, and he caught up to the rest of the gang. And now he's like this really confident outgoing guy who sort of found himself."

Brad's newfound confidence worries Peter—especially knowing that Brad also has a crush on the same girl Peter does—MJ. "He just really wants to get MJ's attention, and this trip for him is the moment—it's his time," says Hii. "Of course, then there's a little bit of a rivalry with Peter at the same time to try and get the girl, so to speak, which is a lot of fun to play around with because I think the dynamic that we have—Tom, Zendaya, and I—I just think that it's a really fun little side plot there."

LEAVING SPIDEY BEHIND

Peter doesn't want to be Spider-Man—at least for a little while. His goals for the summer are much more ordinary. "He's trying to go on vacation with a girl he likes and to hang out with his friends, but he keeps getting wrapped up in these Super Hero adventures along the way," Carroll says. "Where the first movie was about a kid desperate to leave his regular life behind so that he could do more Spider-Man-ing, this one is almost the exact opposite. He's not reluctant to be a hero, but it keeps getting in the way of him telling the girl he likes how he feels or hanging out with his friends on what was supposed to be just this amazing trip to Europe with his class."

Unfortunately for Peter, his aunt, May, decides to pack his Spidey suit in his luggage for him anyway.

MR. HARRINGTON & MR. DELL

Chaperoning the school trip are teachers Mr. Harrington and Mr. Dell. "JB [Smoove] and I get to walk in and play two teachers," says actor Martin Starr. "They're doing their best with kids who are living in a really crazy world with crazy experiences going on around. And we're not so good at helping guide them. But we're trying. . . . We definitely enjoy each other at times. But where some characters have it together, we don't. We're kind of lacking good judgment or intelligence or wisdom."

While Starr returns to reprise his role from the first film, Smoove is a brand-new addition—sort of. Smoove was able to work with Tom Holland's version of Spider-Man during a cross-promotion spot for *Spider-Man: Homecoming* and car company Audi. "Tom Holland and myself, we did a commercial together for the newest Audi, and I played a driving instructor in this commercial," Smoove recalls. "The commercial was fabulous. We had a great time shooting. . . . A year later, [after] this commercial—this amazing commercial—they called me about a role in the new Spider-Man movie. And me and [director] Jon [Watts] talked on the phone. I said, 'Jon, you know I did a commercial last year,' and he said, 'I know. The commercial was great, and that's why we are considering you to come in the new movie.'"

1   Concept illustration by Luke Deering

2   Concept illustration by Tani Kunitake

SPIDER-MAN TAKES EUROPE

1

Spider-Man: Far From Home **takes Spidey global, bringing** him to iconic European cities like Venice, Prague, and London. "The goal is always to try to show people something they've never seen before, and I think an immediate difference in this film compared to any other Spider-Man movie we've seen is we're going to take Peter out of his comfort zone—take him not just out of New York, but take him into Europe," says Watts. "This is a really great way to tell a fish-out-of-water story with Spider-Man."

"One of the really exciting ideas of setting this movie in Europe is not just having Spider-Man try to navigate, say, the canals of Venice, or climb the walls of a castle—all things we've never seen—but also getting to take this group of young kids and put them in places they've never been before—places they're awestruck by, places they're having fun, places they're having fun being in, just looking around," Carroll says. "If you've ever gotten to travel to a place like Europe, and especially if you got to do it when you were really young, it really is magical. It really is this thing where you realize how different other cultures can be and how small differences here and there really add up to make cities like Paris feel completely different than cities like New York."

2

NICK FURY

After some sightseeing in Venice—mixed in with battling a giant watery being—Peter Parker returns to his hotel room to find an unlikely guest waiting for him. "The first time Tom discovers me in this film was a really great moment," says Samuel L. Jackson of his character, Nick Fury. "It was like the first day I worked, and everybody else was like, 'Oh my God, Nick Fury's coming to work today.' But I'm having the same thing with, 'Oh my God, I'm working with Spider-Man today'—which always shocks people that I feel that way."

Spider-Man and Nick Fury both want the same thing, but they each take a different approach to get there. "They want to help people," Carroll says. "They're good guys, but at the same time, Nick Fury might be a little more jaded and willing to go to some further lengths—where Peter Parker is still approaching this as a young kid, a young idealist, who is like, 'No, we don't have to take such drastic measures, perhaps, and we can still get the job done.'"

Although Spider-Man has proven himself capable in the past, Fury hasn't made up his mind about the young hero. "He has serious doubts about Peter," says Samuel L. Jackson. "Number one, Peter is still a kid, and Fury wasn't around when he was in Marvel Studios' *Civil War*. And even though Tony Stark chose him, Fury still has to vet him himself because he always had issues with Stark anyway. So why Stark chose him, he's still trying to figure that particular part of it out."

In the end credit sequence for *Spider-Man: Far From Home*, it is revealed that the real Nick Fury was actually on vacation in space, and the Fury on planet Earth is actually a Skrull—a shapeshifting race of aliens—named Talos impersonating him. Talos, as you might recall, was previously introduced in Marvel Studios' *Captain Marvel*.

1 Nick Fury whisks Peter Parker away on a speedboat to meet his team in concept illustration by Chris Buongiorno

MARIA HILL

Hill has been working alongside Nick Fury since _Marvel's_ _The Avengers_. After being resurrected from her blipped status, Maria Hill is back on the beat as an integral part of Nick Fury's crew. "In this movie, you get to see a little bit of what life is like for us on the road, which you don't really get to see in the other movies because it's not as exciting," says actor Cobie Smulders of her character. "To me, it's very exciting, and I think to the viewers it's going to be interesting seeing these two characters driving to where they're supposed to go to meet with somebody to question them about an event. There's this intimate relationship between the two of them that we've never seen, because we've only really seen them together at high-stakes moments or breaking down the problem of whatever the Super Heroes are going to go and solve, and I think it's very interesting and very human to see these two people just going about their day. It revolves around a lot of drama, but they're used to that and accustomed to it. So, to them, it's just another day at work."

Like Fury, the Maria Hill appearing in _Spider-Man: Far From Home_ is revealed as being impersonated by a Skrull in the end credit scene.

DIMITRI

"We think there's going to be a lot of fun with Spider-Man being pulled into this world, where Fury is introducing him to a bunch of really rough-and-tumble spies," Carroll says. "Where Peter Parker is a little more used to hanging out with the likes of Captain America with his perfect smile and his clean costume, and all of a sudden he's going to be thrown into an adventure with Nick Fury and a bunch of mercenaries."

One of those mercenaries is Dimitri, who impersonates a bus driver hired for Peter's school trip to Prague.

To protect Peter's secret identity, Fury gives him a new tactical suit. "Peter is in Europe," says Meinerding. "He brought his Spider-Man suit with him but is scared to use it on another school field trip with all of his friends around because then they'll know that somebody on the field trip has to be Spider-Man, right? Because it's just too much of a coincidence that Spider-Man is showing up to save that same group of friends. So when Nick Fury enlists him to help out with the elemental crisis, he asks Nick for a suit and Nick's about to turn around a suit in very short order. The suit he gets is meant to look like, more or less, a run-of-the-mill, stock S.H.I.E.L.D. tactical suit of some description."

The final, constructed version of the stealth suit quickly became a favorite of Holland's. "It was nice for me because it's totally different and totally fresh," he says. "It's much comfier than the spandex—and it also looks pretty badass too."

The stealth suit is featured in Peter's fight against the fire elemental. When Betty thinks the dark figure shooting out webs is Spider-Man, Ned denies and deflects, quickly announcing the character as being the Night Monkey—a name that quickly spreads throughout Europe.

1 Spider-Man in his new stealth suit blends right in with
   Fury's crew in concept illustration by Henrik Tamm
2 Character illustration by Ryan Meinerding
3 Stealth suit goggle concepts by Ironhead Studio
4 Character illustration closeup by Ryan Meinerding

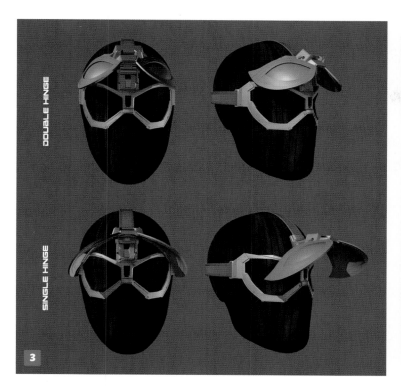

DOUBLE HINGE

SINGLE HINGE

3

RM

4

Quentin Beck—aka Mysterio—introduces himself as a hero from an alternate dimension. Having been part of a task force that fought elemental beings and eventually lost their planet, Beck is now trying to stop that same threat from destroying Peter's home world. Too bad it's all a lie. Beck needs something from Peter and is manipulating him to get what he needs. "What I love about the character of Quentin Beck is that you really never know who he actually is," says actor Jake Gyllenhaal. "I mean, most of the characters in the Marvel Cinematic Universe, even if you're unsure for a while, eventually define themselves. But with Mysterio, his name is so apt. I don't think you ever really know who he is even in the end, and I love that."

"It was so much fun to see how excited he got about the idea of bringing this particular guy to the screen, and the duality that he has," Carroll says of Gyllenhaal. "Because Jake has done these roles where he plays the really sincere, really good guy, and he's also played these roles like in *Nightcrawler* where he's a legitimately frightening personality—and one of the things that makes Quentin Beck, or Mysterio, so cool is that he has to be both. He has to be the charming con man that you want to hand over the keys to the kingdom to, but at the same time he has to be a very serious threat to our hero."

Key to Mysterio's hero design was translating the comic version into a believable part of the MCU—fishbowl-shaped helmet and all. "From my point of view, I always wanted to do Mysterio as Mysterio was in the comics," Meinerding says. "He's one of those characters that when you saw him in the comics, he's weird, it's different. No one's going to copy that character and get away with it. [Comic book artist] Steve Ditko carved out a niche for that visual that is not really going to be copied again. So to try to translate that to the screen, for me it was always going to have to be, 'How do we get the fishbowl? How do we make it interesting in some way as opposed to just being a glass reflective ball or something?' In the comics, it's depicted a number of different ways. Sometimes he's like a shadowy head inside. Sometimes it looks like it's smoke. Sometimes it just looks like it's frosted."

Knowing Beck's hidden scheme, Meinerding pulled ideas from already established characters for Mysterio's design. If Beck was going to pretend to be a hero and take inspiration for his

1 Nick Fury meets Mysterio in concept illustration by Randolph Watson

2 Mysterio helmet illustration by Ryan Meinerding

3 Mysterio character illustration by Ryan Meinerding

costume from various MCU heroes, then the filmmaking team needed to follow the exact same process. "He's creating a persona for himself," Meinerding says. "He's looking at other heroes and saying, 'Oh, I want to be a little bit of Iron Man, a little bit of Doctor Strange, a little bit of Thor,' and wrapping that all into one thing. I did a big, mechanical-suit version that looks like an Iron Man suit that has the fishbowl. I did a version of him in a skintight, Vision-looking suit, and then some of the other ones started to become mixes. It started to work a little bit better when we were mixing that technology with the mystical, magical stuff—Thor mixed with Doctor Strange mixed with Iron Man. Some of them went more technological; some of them went more Super Hero; some of them went in other directions. When we started combining the heroes, it made a little bit more sense. . . . I think people are used to the heroes, they're used to heightened visuals, and they're used to heightened costumes. So if we just say that this is a new look for a hero, I think most people would like to buy into it. Their suspension of disbelief is going to stretch out a little further than it used to."

With a design in place, the process turned to the costume's actual construction. "Once you get those cool drawings from Ryan Meinerding, there's always a little bit of a fear that it won't translate to reality," Carroll says. "But [Costume Designer] Anna B. Sheppard and her team with [Costume FX Supervisor] Graham Churchyard and [Associate Costume Designer] Michael Mooney nailed it. It looks so cool. It's just as impressive in person as it is on camera. It's got all these practical lights in it, even in the cape. It's astounding."

1 3D model of Mysterio's helmet by Adam Ross

3 Character illustration by Ryan Meinerding

2 Character illustration by Ryan Meinerding

4 Character illustration of Quentin Beck by Ryan Meinerding

Beck is not the hero he claims to be. In reality he is a dis-gruntled former employee of Stark Enterprises. "Probably the trickiest part of this film was trying to figure out Mysterio's turn," Tom Holland says. "Obviously, the Spider-Man fans who read the comics will know that Mysterio is a villain. So for us, it was really trying to get the audience to forget about that during the film and then really punch them in the stomach with the reality that he's been playing Peter this entire time. And for us, that was the most complicated part."

Filmmakers considered various ideas depicting how Mysterio crafted his illusions, but one stood out to them. "I pitched the idea of him essentially being in a mocap suit and that whatever technology he had could read the pattern. Anything that had the mocap pattern on it would be read and then erased from the illusion," Meinerding says. "[President of Marvel Studios and Chief Creative Officer of Marvel] Kevin [Feige] gravitated toward that, and then it started going down that road of making it actually look like characters that we replace in our own movies."

To create the illusions, Beck uses Stark technology weaponized drones integrated with a holographic system of his own design. "Very early in the process, we knew there were going to be drones and we knew that they were going to be controlled by Mysterio," Meinerding says. "And in order to communicate that big idea to all

the producers who were working on the film, I did a series of illustrations showing what everybody would see and then repainting the illustration with what's actually there. So I have a few concepts with drones—not as threatening-looking as the drones finally designed by Josh Nizzi—but drones that were supposed to have been projecting things with Mysterio controlling them."

"The drones are based on a Stark design but modified with special patterns similar to motion-capture suits used in film," concept illustrator Josh Nizzi says. "These markings allow a computer to track the location and orientation of an object in space, making it possible to digitally alter or remove them altogether. . . . The director wanted the drone to look intimidating and bulky, something that could do real damage to whatever it crashed into. It also needed to be loaded with many different types of weapons that could cause all types of destruction."

1   Character illustration of Quentin Beck's mocap suit by Ryan Meinerding
2   3D model of Quentin Beck's helmet display by Adam Ross
3   Concept illustration of Quentin Beck's mobile remote by Kamen Anev
4   Character illustration of Quentin Beck commanding drones by Ryan Meinerding

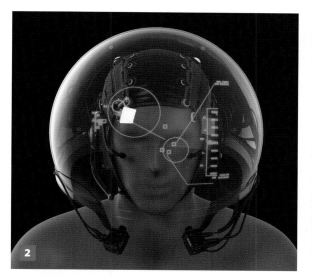

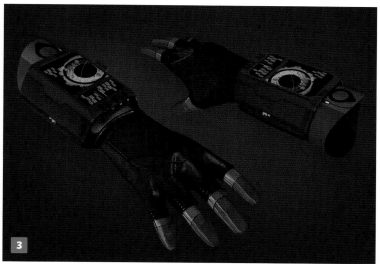

- TRACKING MARKERS ADDED TO LEGS
- PADDED VEST TO LOOK PROTECTIVE
- HOLSTER + GUN ADDED
- GRENADES ADDED

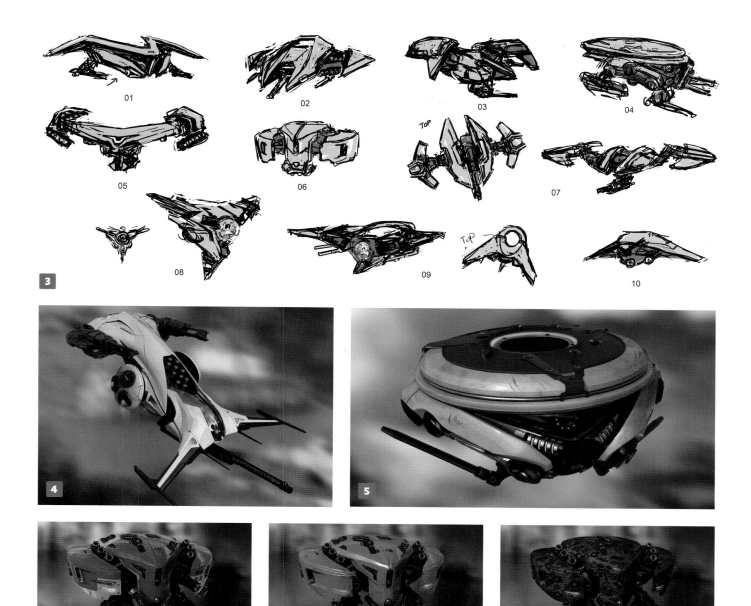

1 Early concept illustration of Quentin Beck controlling mobile drones by Ryan Meinerding

2 Concept illustration of Quentin Beck controlling mobile drones by Ryan Meinerding

3 Drone concept sketches by Josh Nizzi

4 Early drone concept illustration by Josh Nizzi

5 Early drone concept illustration by Josh Nizzi

6 Drone concept illustration with Iron Man painted exterior by Josh Nizzi

7 Drone concept illustration with dark grey painted exterior by Josh Nizzi

8 Drone concept illustration with tracking markers on exterior by Josh Nizzi

9 Drone concept illustration with tracking markers on exterior by Josh Nizzi

Mysterio isn't working alone. "Quentin Beck has a crew of people that hate Iron Man," Holland says. "Beck, furthermore, used to work for Iron Man and actually invented the B.A.R.F. technology, which Iron Man displays in Marvel Studios' *Civil War*, and that's partly to do with the technology used in this movie to convince the world of the threat. So yeah, his crew—his little motley crew—is built up with people that Tony Stark has upset throughout the years."

Beck and his team practice and carefully choreograph the drone movement and planned destruction for the global threat. These illusions need to feel real. For the monsters that Beck and his crew had designed, filmmakers were able to tip their hat to various villains found throughout Spider-Man's history. "There are a lot of really cool Spider-Man villains from the comics who have not been translated to film yet," says head of visual development Ryan Meinerding. "We were looking to places where we could bring those characters to the screen—characters who would never really get a fair shake otherwise, like Hydro-Man and Molten Man—and make them related to each other in the sense that they came from another dimension. It seemed like a fun way of transitioning characters from the comics."

Although the elemental beings are holographic projections in the film's plot, all of the creatures were animated on film using CGI.

1   Concept illustration by Jackson Sze
2   Concept illustration by Anthony Francisco
3   Concept illustration by Anthony Francisco
4   Concept illustration by Anthony Francisco
5   Concept illustration by Randolph Watson

Hearing that the small Mexican village of Ixtenco was destroyed by a cyclone with a face, Nick Fury and Maria Hill decide to investigate the claims. While there, they meet Quentin Beck—and a giant creature composed entirely of earth.

Concept artist Jerad Marantz tapped into his vast design experience when conceptualizing not only the earthen creature, but all the other elemental beings seen in *Spider-Man: Far From Home*. "I'm a creature guy," Marantz says. "I've been doing creature design for close to 20 years now, and I've had the pleasure of working on character, creature, and costume designs while at Marvel. But for this film, [Head of Visual Development] Ryan [Meinerding] brought me on because I have an extensive creature background. This is where he needed me, and it was a blast to just take on all of these elemental creatures."

As earth can take on many different forms—like rock, dirt, and sand—Marantz was able to interpret the earth elemental in mul-

tiple ways. "I ran the gamut from being very solid, to being made of mud and grass and roots, to being made out of boulders—and then with earlier versions, it was huge," he says. "A lot of it was material exploration. Eventually, for my final pass on the character, it was about dirt and wind and showing that motion, having the boulders floating and actually being connected by dust, and having a character who could expand and contract its shape based on what it was doing. That last pass was all about movement."

1   Character sketches by Jerad Marantz
2   Character illustrations by Jerad Marantz
3   Character illustrations by Jerad Marantz
4   Character illustration by Jerad Marantz

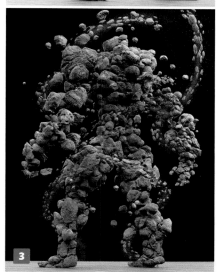

Following an off-camera attack by an air elemental in Morocco, a third elemental (albeit the second shown on-screen) emerges from the canals of Venice, Italy. This one is composed entirely of water.

When filmmakers decided to have Spider-Man face off against Hydro-Man, Venice seemed like the perfect location for the battle. "We've been excited to shoot in Venice since we first had the idea, which was way back early on in script development," Carroll says. "Spider-Man in the comics has this great villain called Hydro-Man. He's a lesser-known guy when you compare him to the Vultures of the world, but he's a really interesting character who has persevered in comics for decades, and we think that's because he's got this really interesting power set. Spider-Man can't just punch him. Spider-Man can't just web him up. He's made of water. So we thought the idea of having Spider-Man face off with Hydro-Man right here in Venice, Italy, was a really cool idea."

For designing the water-based creature, Marantz's earlier concepts looked much closer to the Hydro-Man source inspiration than the final designs seen on-screen. "There was an idea of him in a containment suit, like a science experiment gone wrong,"

Marantz says. "That's right out of the comic. Any version where he had hair, we were going right out of the comic for that." Designing a humanoid shape made of water proved challenging but was made easier through the use of computer software. "In the initial pass, I did everything as 2D in Photoshop," Marantz says. "It was just Photoshop and line work. And then once [head of visual development] Ryan [Meinerding] approved a direction, I started resolving the character in 3D. It became much easier to sculpt the water and render out the material to make it appear like it was actually water. Then I painted in more of the movement, and added more of the spray and more of the kinetic energy of the actual waves."

1 Concept illustration by Ryan Meinerding

2 Character illustration by Jerad Marantz

3 Character illustration by Jerad Marantz

4 Character illustration by Jerad Marantz

5 Character illustration by Jerad Marantz

6 Character illustration by Jerad Marantz

1

Bubbling up to the surface beneath a fountain in Prague, the next element-based creature reveals itself. This time, it's made entirely of molten lava. "In the beginning, I did a lot of experimentation with the material," concept artist Jerad Marantz says of designing Molten Man. "I was trying to find a way to create something that implied movement even though it was still on a stagnant sculpt. So you can see a lot of swirling and breaking-up patterns as if areas of the body are cool and warm and very much like magma in areas—so dark and light areas. You can see different types of material studies—like steel going from cool to actually having the heat underneath it, so the surface of it is cooler than what's going on. But we ended up resting with a consistent, liquid-y, molten character."

In the script, Molten Man becomes more powerful as it latches onto metallic objects, melting them down and growing larger. This plot point informed a lot of what would be the character's final design. "We ended up going more amorphous because as he would walk by or go over metal objects, he would absorb them and become bigger and bigger and bigger—adding to him," Marantz says. "So that's why in the later versions you see cars and steel beams stuck in him. And as he would move forward, that would just kind of seep in and contribute to his mass—so he would get really big."

Although filmmakers used the city of Prague leading up this fiery encounter, Peter's battle against Molten Man was actually filmed in another Czech town—Liberec.

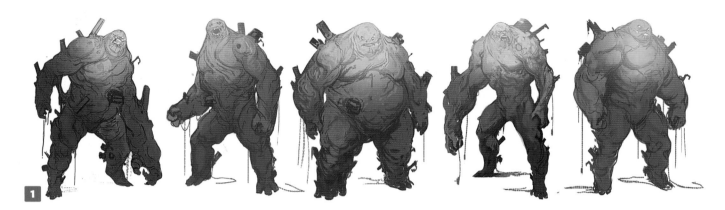

2

3

1   Character sketches by Jerad Marantz

2   Character illustration by Jerad Marantz

3   Concept illustration by Henrik Tamm

4   Concept illustration by Ryan Meinerding

5   Molten Man emerges from metal statue in
    3D concepts by Jerad Marantz

6   Concept illustration by Henrik Tamm

4

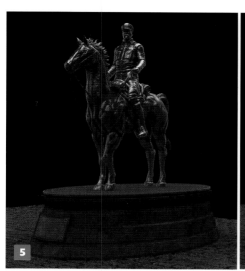

Needing to stage an Avengers-level threat for the final piece of their plan, Beck and his crew create a mega-creature. Taking the four elements they had already used—earth, air, water, and fire—the Elemental Illusions are combined to create one giant beast.

"The approach was to find a way to blend all of them together, and what we ended up with was water tendrils and molten body, and then the smoke that comes off of the molten body is the wind," Marantz says. "The idea was to have all of them combined into one Super Elemental. It becomes this ultimate threat. It was just trying to find a convincing way to combine all of them in a dynamic, mega-monster."

1 Spider-Man catches a ride to the Super Elemental in concept illustration by Henrik Tamm

2 Character illustration by Jerad Marantz

3 Character illustration by Jerad Marantz

4 Character illustration by Jerad Marantz

ILLUSION BATTLE

After helping Mysterio defeat Molten Man in Prague, MJ helps Peter uncover a larger plot. Quentin Beck is not who he says he is. Peter ditches his school group and heads to Berlin to tell Fury what he's discovered. Sadly, he never gets the chance.

Intercepted by Quentin Beck and his crew, Beck plays with Peter's sense of reality in order to learn what he knows, and who he's told. Running a gauntlet of artificial imagery, Peter struggles to understand what is real and what is not.

To animate the mostly CGI sequence, filmmakers turned to visual effects company Framestore—which also worked on some of the mesmerizing sequences from Marvel Studios' *Doctor Strange*. While oftentimes vfx (visual effects) vendors are asked to execute an already-established directorial vision, for the Illusion Battle, director Jon Watts only had one request—to make it weird. This allowed Framestore not only to create the visual effects for the sequence, but to design the imagery as well.

Under the guidance of filmmakers like Watts and vfx supervisor Janek Sirrs, Framestore conceptualized a number of surrealistic environments and psychedelic imagery for Peter to be thrown into. In the final sequence, audiences glimpse a punishing duality—as Mysterio's vivid imagery

tears at Peter mentally, his illusions hide real-world objects that hurt him physically.

While most of the sequence was fully CG, some plates—live action footage that has CGI applied to it—were used. Framestore also utilized mocap reference of Tom Holland to help animate the digital Spider-Man's movements. Overall, the illusion battle had around 140 vfx shots in the entire mind-bending sequence.

1 Quentin Beck pretends to be Nick Fury in concept illustration by Damien Carr

2 Concept illustration by Ryan Meinerding

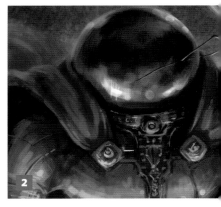

1	Concept illustration by Tani Kunitake	**5**	Concept illustration by Randolph Watson
2	Concept illustration by Henrik Tamm	**6**	Concept illustration by Henrik Tamm
3	Concept illustration by Tani Kunitake	**7**	Concept illustration by Henrik Tamm
4	Concept illustration by Henrik Tamm	**8**	Concept illustration by Tani Kunitake

ATTACK IN VENICE

Peter Parker's first stop in Europe is the beautiful city of Venice, Italy—where he immediately comes face to face with a giant watery being. "Not even an hour after he gets to Venice, this crazy event happens where Hydro-Man comes up out of nowhere and starts wreaking havoc," Carroll says. "And of course, he's got to intervene as Spider-Man—but there's also this crazy introduction of this new hero he's never met before."

For filming, production traveled to the city of canals to capture as much footage as possible. "Shooting a movie in Venice is like shooting nowhere else on Earth," Carroll says. "It's literally a city built in the middle of the ocean on stilts, and you have to get everywhere by boat or foot. Movies rely on trucks and being able to cart all the equipment around on those massive trucks, but we can't do that here. . . . It's literally going to be men and women carrying this stuff over these bridges, through these canals, and on gondolas."

While in the city, filmmakers relied on drones to help get dynamic, aerial shots. "It used to be that if you wanted to get these beautiful aerial shots, you had to have this giant heli-

copter, you have to have a crew of several people—some of whom are in charge of flying the helicopter, the rest in charge of running the specialized cameras attached to that helicopter," Carroll explains. "But now you can get this amazing aerial footage with these tiny devices and these amazing little cameras. There are a lot of restrictions on it though—in a lot of places—but Venice is one of the very few places where they're very open to that but because of course, it's all over canals so worst-case scenario these drones go down, they go down in the river."

For scenes too dangerous or technical to be filmed in Venice, namely the ones with Hydro-Man, filmmakers replicated parts of the city at Leavesden Studios just outside of London. "We had to build the Rialto Bridge," production designer Claude Paré says. "But in three separate elements: One in the giant tank that exists in Leavesden Studios and two other elements that were dry docks for facility of shooting. We scouted Venice many times, and we grabbed the best elements that we could compose into one set. And with visual effects, we had to also make sure that everything that

would be assembled together would be able to be plated and scanned and used later on [during post-production] to augment the set."

Even though the final Hydro-Man was crafted using CGI, not all water effects were digital. Filmmakers tried to capture as many practical effects as possible. "We spent the whole week on this massive Venice set we built on the back lot over this giant water tank so we could actually do the water effects—throw people in the water, have giant waves every-where," Carroll says. "And there was Tom himself on wires, running across things over the top of the water, pretending to pole-vault up onto the iconic Rialto Bridge. It's just so much fun to watch him do all this stuff himself."

1   The canals of Venice recreated at Leavesden Studios
2   The canals of Venice recreated at Leavesden Studios

1   The canals of Venice recreated at
    Leavesden Studios
2   Concept illustration by Phil Langone
3   Concept illustration by Damien Carr

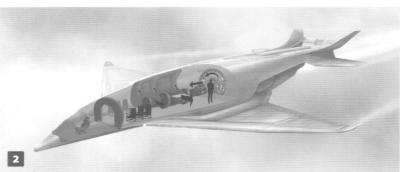

"After Berlin, it seems like he's really in trouble," Carroll says of Peter. "He is stranded in the Netherlands with no vehicle, no phone, and no ID. He couldn't even get home if he wanted to. Luckily, he manages to get ahold of Happy, who shows up in one of Tony's jets."

Now united with Happy, Peter checks Flash's social media and finds out his friends are in London. "Peter doesn't know what Mysterio is planning next, but he does know that he wants to kill his friends, since they could expose Mysterio," says Carroll.

While Happy flies the Stark jet toward London, Peter works to create a brand-new Spidey suit by using the secret workshop in the back of the plane. He'll need a new one for the impending battle. "The suit is an amazing reveal and kind of an homage to the first [Marvel Studios'] *Iron Man* in the way that it's made," Holland says. "I actually was watching a specific scene from that film, trying to mimic Robert's movements as exactly as I could. Whether or not that reads on camera, I don't know—but I hope it does because it was a real nice detail that [director] Jon [Watts] and I came up with. And for the real hardcore fans, they're really, really going to appreciate that sort of acknowledgment and respect to the godfather of the MCU."

"There are a few cool things about the suit that Peter builds for himself in the lab on the jet that Happy arrives in," Carroll explains. "First and foremost, it is the first high-tech suit that Peter designs for himself so it has a few really striking visual differences. Peter ditches the blue of his original sweatsuit costume, and the first suit Tony made for him, and replaces it with a really slick-looking black. There is also this big, bold white version of the spider symbol on his back, which is really iconic. Peter also infused the suit with some unique tech. To make the suit more durable, it is woven from threads made from his web-fluid tech. This makes the suit thinner, lighter, and a lot stronger."

Peter also designs his own version of the web-wings created in the MCU by Tony Stark—and in the comics by artist Steve Ditko for Spider-Man's first appearance in 1962's *Amazing Fantasy* #15. While a smaller version of the web-wings can be seen in *Spider-Man: Homecoming*, a much larger version that gives Peter the ability to glide is seen in the *Far From Home* final battle.

For filming, physical suits were created. These Spider-Man costumes are a very challenging, technical suit to construct. Add in multiple versions—from fully clean to battle worn—and it becomes quite a task to manufacture exactly what you need. "I

think what we'll have learned working on this is it's probably one of the hardest costumes you could work," costume fx supervisor Graham Churchyard says. "I think because of it, you're trying to achieve a seamless, wrinkle-free costume—and obviously visual effects pick up in post-production and help us fix things—but as much as possible, you know? Twenty people for six months worked on these costumes, and not just one [suit], obviously. There are many repeats and different changes for Spider-Man. It's just a huge task taking the concept, lifting it off the page, and turning it into a costume."

"It is like wearing a work of art," Holland says of his final hero suit. "They are so realistic, and they look exactly like you'd imagine them out of the comics that it's almost disappointing that you're not Spider-Man. It looks so realistic that it feels like you should be able to climb walls and you should be able to shoot webs."

1 Stark jet vehicle concept by Dan Walker

2 Stark jet layout concept by Henrik Tamm

3 Set illustrations by Henrik Tamm

4 Spider-Man suit gag concept by Rodney Fuentebella

1 Web-wing concept
illustrations by Ryan
Meinerding

2 An earlier version of
Spider-Man's web-wings
as conceptualized by
Rodney Fuentebella for
Spider-Man: Homecoming

SWINGING THROUGH LONDON

FOR THE FINAL BATTLE IN *SPIDER-MAN: FAR FROM Home*, Peter Parker finds himself in London. However, this isn't the first time the web-slinging hero has fought in the British capital. As always, filmmakers found inspiration in the comics. "The beginning of the big climax of the movie is awesome because it's straight out of the comics," Carroll says. "*Amazing Spider-Man* #95 from 1971 is literally Spider-Man swinging across Tower Bridge in the middle of this crazy action sequence."

1 Cover from *Amazing Spider-Man* #95 (1971) written by Stan Lee and penciled by John Romita Sr.

ANATOMY OF A SCENE

LONDON ATTACK

Peter Parker has figured out Beck is a villain and has been staging these attacks to make Mysterio seem like a hero. Now, Peter must come up with a plan for how to stop him and save his friends. "He has a rough idea of how Beck's tech works," says Carroll of Spider-Man. "So he's racking his brain trying to think of ways to disrupt the illusions and reveal Mysterio for the fraud he is—but he also knows that Mysterio's tech is really powerful, so it's not going to be easy."

The final sequence in London starts off like any other attack, but once Spider-Man is able to stop the illusion, the battle transforms into something new and unexpected. "This film has a really fun theme that is almost poking fun at the sorts of plots that are in big movies, especially like those in the MCU," says Carroll. "So we knew we had to deliver all the spectacle people expect in a big Super Hero movie finale, but we also wanted it to have this other layer—the layer that would subvert those same expectations, but hopefully in a way that surprises and delights the audience. It had to be huge, but Peter also has to pull the curtain back to reveal that it is all smoke and mirrors. However, once the smoke and mirrors are revealed, that still had to feel like a huge third act too. In the end, I think the result is a pretty interesting finale that people won't expect, even once they know Mysterio is the real antagonist of this film."

To film the battle, actor Tom Holland had to use his imagination to visualize where the fully CGI drones would be in the final, animated sequence. "It was a really complicated scene to shoot because, obviously, what I'm fighting in that sequence doesn't exist," Holland recalls. "So, it was lots of me doing choreographed fight scenes by myself punching thin air. And you feel like an idiot when you do that stuff. You're wearing a Spider-Man suit—it's as form-fitting as a suit can be—and you're punching imaginary drones and then getting shot by imaginary drones.... And when you watch that [final] sequence it looks so cool. And, for the life of me, I can't understand how it looks so cool because it felt so stupid. But it was a really tough scene for me. I felt quite sort of exposed because it just looks so lame on the day. But when [VFX Supervisor] Janek [Sirrs] does his magic and adds in all the effects and stuff it looks awesome. And I'm so glad that [Director] Jon [Watts] kept pushing me to really give it everything I had because it really pays off. And it's really a special moment in our arc of Spider-Man."

For everything too dangerous or impossible to film, CGI was used, with many of Spider-Man's movements being derived from Tom Holland's mocap stage sessions.

1 Mysterio fights the super elemental in concept illustration by Henrik Tamm

2 Drones inside the super elemental are webbed by Spider-Man to help him pull apart Mysterio's illusion in concept illustration by Henrik Tamm

3 Spider-Man fights Quentin Beck's drones in concept illustration by Henrik Tamm

2

3

MARVEL STUDIOS

SPIDER-MAN

No Way Home

2021

Spider-Man is the only Super Hero in the MCU with a secret identity—or at least he was. That all changed during the mid-credits sequence in *Spider-Man: Far From Home*. In that sequence, Spider-Man and MJ, who are hanging out in New York City, turn to watch a breaking news story on a digital billboard screen showing what they know to be altered footage of real events. The video, which was released on the contentious digital news website *The Daily Bugle*, not only blamed Spider-Man for the drone attack in London and the death of the "hero" Mysterio, but outed the man behind the webbed mask.

With Spidey's true identity no longer secret, everyone on the planet now knows that Peter Parker is Spider-Man. "We don't really know what the Spider-Man world is just yet, but what I can say is it's part of this much bigger world, which is the MCU," says Holland. "And it's such an amazing blanket to have because you can draw on so many different movies that have been so successful prior to the one that you're making."

Spider-Man's suits as featured in *Spider-Man: No Way Home*

Concept illustration by Ryan Meinerding

AFTERWORD
THE FUTURE OF SPIDER-MAN

"You know, we've been saying this, how cool would it be if Spider-Man could be a part of our universe—and now he is a part of our universe," says Alonso. "So, be careful what you wish for. Now we have to do it right, and we have to make sure that everything we said we would do way back when that we get to do it, because now we get a chance. So, we're incredibly excited. We understand the responsibility, and we hope we make our fans proud."

For the filmmakers, this is not a task taken lightly, as the weight of expectations from millions of fans around the world rests on their shoulders.

ACKNOWLEDGMENTS

Thank you to everyone at Marvel Studios for helping to make this publication a reality, especially Eric H. Carroll and Ryan Meinerding. Eric: Your kindness and generosity make every book you are part of—including this one—all the better for it. Ryan: I would be hard-pressed to find someone else more dedicated and passionate about Spider-Man than you, and it is easily seen in your beautiful concept designs found throughout this book.

To the amazing filmmakers on all sides of these movies— Marvel, Sony, or otherwise. Thank you to Russ Busse, Andrew Smith, and the rest of the team at Abrams for putting this book together. To my entire support system, especially my mom, my brother James, and Alex. Thank you for always being in my corner. To my dad who I know would be proud of everything I have, and have yet to accomplish.

And to the fans of Spider-Man—past, present, and future— your love of Spidey makes all of this possible.

Eleni Roussos